KARMIC RELATIONSHIPS

KARMIC RELATIONSHIPS

Martin Schulman

SAMUEL WEISER, INC.
York Beach, Maine

First published in 1984 by
Samuel Weiser, Inc.
Box 612
York Beach, Maine 03910

Second Printing 1985

ISBN 0-87728-508-X

Library of Congress Catalog Card Number: 84-51376

Typeset in 11 point Times Roman by
Upright Type
Printed in the United States by
Mitchell-Shear, Inc., Ann Arbor, Michigan

CONTENTS

. . . To those who long for the opportunity to share life's path with another . . .

. . . To those whose boundless love has carried others . . .

. . . To Diane, light as the air, deep as the river, firm as the earth, and gentle as the willow . . . for she guides me to see the unseen . . .

. . . To my dearest Princess Penny Sue, with warmth in her heart, understanding in her mind, and a deep love for all humanity, as she begins her journey into womanhood . . .

. . . To those wonderful students everywhere who drink deeper from the well of knowledge and understanding as they move closer to the fountain of love.

KARMIC RELATIONSHIPS

INTRODUCTION

What is a relationship? What do individuals experience in relationships? What makes relationships form or end? These are the questions that people ask themselves as they search for better ways of finding integration with others. Some involvements are karmic while others are not. We sometimes observe partnerships where the burden of responsibility seems to be carried by one person. In some instances we notice an air of mystery in the way people in a relationship react to each other—a mystery that is difficult to comprehend.

The nature of a relationship may encompass many levels—some conscious, some subliminal. Hidden motivations and karmic lessons often lurk just below the threshold of consciousness. As a result, partners spend a lot of time and effort trying to smooth out these rough spots which are not always obvious. Each individual has many facets of personality which mesh and blend with the qualities of another and ultimately define the overall "relationship."

People get along with each other easily in some areas while experiencing great difficulty in others. Sometimes difficult areas can be overcome or even overlooked if the intrinsic quality of the total relationship is rewarding.

We can cope with what we know but we have no way of understanding what we don't know. Whether or not a relationship will work smoothly is not as important as understanding the constructive and not so constructive energies available. The astrological aspects symbolize the ebb and flow of currents that move between individuals. We can see how the river of understanding winds its way towards enlightenment, and we can view the nooks, crannies and dark corners that must be investigated in order to get the most out of our relationships.

It is important to accept the fact that not all relationships work. Yet they all do exist for a reason, and when we understand more about why a relationship exists, we can better understand ourselves. Some relationships seem to be karmic in nature, others seem more physical or emotional. As we study about the various aspects between two people's charts, the push and pull of the tide of love reveals how our emotional ties are actually mirrors of our forming consciousness.

LOVE:
THE COMPATIBLE IDEAL

One of the greatest mysteries of life is the experience of loving another person. For eons, people have tried to define and understand the depths of love's simplicity. We know the intimate love of one person to another. We experience a love for nature. We have a love for material things. We feel the love for family and children. We have been enveloped by the love for God and for life itself. These are all different forms of love and yet in subtle, intangible ways, they are all the same. A thread of continuity links all forms of love together, so the differences are based more on the love object and the quality of love itself rather than in the basic essence. We know that when one person feels love for another he is able to feel love for other things in the universe because the love center is open. When an individual feels a great love for life, he is capable of loving all things—for loving anything is the foundation for loving everything!

The contemporary definition of love may be confusing. We sometimes confuse passion with love because we misunderstand the difference between sex drive and feeling. Passion excites the personality. Love makes the spirit soar. Passion is power. Love is the only power that can overcome passion. When people relate only through passion they may experience such a volatile sequence of emotions, all ethics and conscience is thrown to the winds. Love is far less exciting, but has immeasurably more value, for its essence is a quiet sustaining force that wells up from the soul, filling and soothing the empty spaces in one's being, as it brings an individual a sense of completion.

It has been said that "time heals all wounds." This is not necessarily true for many people spend years dwelling on past hurts. Love is the true healer. Even Jesus, whose love was so great that he sought harmony with all of mankind, never healed unless he felt love. The power of love is unquestionably the greatest power on this earth. As we search for reasons for existence, we sometimes strain our intellect in order to understand our place in the universe. We need only experience love to fully appreciate divine purpose. Where reason and logic end, love begins.

Love nourishes the spirit, and it feeds the soul. Love is the difference between a musical note and hearing music. It creates a gratitude for life that emanates from the very core of an individual's soul, blossoming into the feeling that everything is going to be all right.

Because people try to simplify feelings, we have come to believe that love and hate are two opposing ideas, or two sides of the same coin. However, people whose hearts are filled with love are incapable of hate. Those whose hearts are filled with hate cannot even know that love exists. Instead of love and hate being opposites of each other, they are really so different we can't find the pure essence of both in the same individual. Love is that which makes all things come together. Its true meaning is not easily verbalized. It could be compared to a light that glows within the seed of truth, bringing warmth and divine inspiration to all who are able to perceive its essence. Love has the power to put together the puzzle of life, solving the riddles of the mind and giving purpose to seemingly unrelated experiences. It is the one force that makes man harmonious with himself.

When an individual can achieve a harmonious under-standing of himself, he tends to grow more harmonious with all the love that is in the world. He can start walking the path of becoming a divinely spiritual being. The study of astrological compatibility can help us on the path, for the chart itself points the way to understanding how much we are a part of the divine force which is guiding and moving our lives. No one can experience love with another and be out of tune with himself.

When one person completes himself through loving another, a third factor comes into play. The universe seems to bend itself to meet and fulfill the goals of both. Difficult situations become easy. Obstacles seem to miraculously melt away. A deep sense of purpose begins to blossom from two stems intertwining towards a universal oneness. When we realize that love manifests through art, music, poetry, form, design, feeling, nature, wisdom and all levels of under-standing, then it becomes easy to see how relationships, or the finding and sharing of love with another, are truly the jewels of life.

Karmic Relationships

All relationships contain opportunities for personal growth. They afford the obstacles and rewards, the pitfalls and pinnacles, the personal participation experience that shows us how we cope with our life philosophy when we have to live what we preach. When karma is involved we tend to feel a lack of control over the circumstances and events that occur, as well as a lack of control over how we react to these events. A person may see himself acting somewhat out-of-character when he is fulfilling and correcting certain past-life qualities connected to a personality with which he is no longer consciously familiar. Karmically, these qualities must be evolved if the individual is to grow more in contact with his present life. The karmic relationship takes on the tone of each individual, while stripping away the illusions of the other. Through this process, new awarenesses are reached and a sense of lightness and freedom can be experienced as the burden of karmic weight is being released. Interestingly enough, the karmic pattern is usually understood clearly *only after a lesson has been learned!*

An individual can struggle through difficulties in a relationship for months or years without even realizing what the struggle is all about. Only after the underlying difficulty has surfaced and been solved does the karmic burden actually dissolve. The reward for the hard work is understanding, and it comes after we realize the interwoven link between past life residue and NOW!

Karma tends to be expressed through a string of similar experiences that manifest over a period of years. When we enter a relationship, it is often because we unconsciously see something in the other individual which can help us to resolve a karmic problem. In other words, we attract who we need at a time in our life when we are ready to understand. Thus, the ancient adage, "When the student is ready, the teacher is there," is truly the characteristic tone of why and how karmic relationships occur.

Personal Growth Relationships

A flower blooms when it is ready. The petals open in season revealing the great mystery of the blossom. The miracle of birth takes place after months of preparation. Similarly, the revelations that come from karmic understanding also have a period of gestation. We are not usually ready to resolve karmic lessons; we are usually at the stage of gathering information. Sometimes this "forming" process takes us through years of experiencing one involvement after another—for these temporary or intermediate personal growth relationships provide the basic insights that pave the way for future resolution of karmic patterns. Like the embryo in the womb, these short term relationships represent the foundation providing the necessary rungs on the evolutionary ladder that we climb in our search for a better life.

Unlike the karmic relationship, the lessons that can be learned do not appear in sequential order, but they will represent parts of the puzzle whose shape is not yet defined.

Often, one difficulty or obstacle is solved only to be replaced by another. One lesson can be understood and then we find it does little to improve the total relationship. This kind of experience occurs when we cannot relate to another because we have not yet faced the truth of ourselves. The solving of these relating problems through the mastering of obstacles helps us to get ready to accept the karmic insights that will come later. Personal growth relationships offer a vehicle by which emotions, ideas, and attitudes must be worked through on a day to day basis so that every inch of "personality" soil can be tilled before the spiritual garden grows.

The Unconscious Anima and Animus

Life's appearances often hide the true stream of consciousness which is the source of our action. We admire the beauty of a tree and never notice its roots. These very roots, hidden in the soil, produce the life essence of the tree. Subtleties that occur in relationships come from the roots of that relationship. We see their manifestations as the branches of the tree. The way in which the roots grow will determine the strength and direction of the branches. The roots of any relationship are nourished by the unconscious qualities and patterns developed through years and lifetimes. Carl Jung, the noted psychologist, spoke of the anima and animus figures in the unconscious. He thought they were two sides of the same source of unconscious development. These symbols are extremely important when we try to understand what actually happens in human interaction.

Sigmund Freud noted that a male child first learns about love from his mother. As the child grows, he retains the unconscious memories of her love as a symbol or model of what he will ultimately seek from a relationship. Through the years fragments are added to this unconscious picture in a similar manner to the tree annually growing more roots. As more impressions are collected from the various people who show the individual love, he begins to slowly fill in the details of what he will come to need in a companion. Perhaps a female teacher with dark hair rewarded him for a scholarly achievement. He may unconsciously remember dark haired females as somehow enhancing his intellectual abilities. Perhaps at some time a woman with a soothing voice calms him from some temporary fear. He may remember this tone of voice as being symbolic of a sense of security. At another time he may meet a woman who gives him the care and attention he needs. Her characteristics are added to the unconscious construct of his "perfect woman" image. The unconscious needs of each person develop naturally, much as the roots of the tree grow in the direction promising the most water and nourishment. When all the different aspects of love, protection and strength are gathered together, the "anima" figure is formed. From this construct the male develops his taste for what he wants of a female companion. And he will compare any woman he relates to with this image.

The female builds a similar type of construct. She will collect the qualities of males, including the father, who have shown her love during her childhood years and she forms her unconscious "animus" figure. In any relationship she forms she will compare the real life qualities of the male to this idealized conception.

The tree grows from a tiny seed. Although thousands of oak seeds will produce thousands of oak trees, each tree will be different because its growth is influenced by its nourishment. It will express the individualistic characteristics of the seed it came from because an oak cannot become a maple. And the roots of this tree are influenced by conditions which existed prior to birth.

Carl Jung noted that fragments of the anima and animus figures come from common mythic images. It could also be that unconscious memories of past-life loves may be brought into this life with the expectation of finding the same qualities again. Strong past-life residue may affect the development of the anima or animus figure. This phenomenon may cause a person to attract a "karmic" relationship in the present incarnation.

When people are unable to find the anima-animus qualities in a mate, they over-identify with these qualities within themselves. In this way, they play both roles. When a woman also plays the role of a man or when a man acts out feminine qualities in addition to his role, the relationship can get very confused. And, not uncommonly, these people may not even be aware that the confusion is coming from images within.

Role Playing

We enter each relationship with different expectations. Sometimes we hope to achieve security or enduring love or the recognition of our existence, or even confirmation of our life's outlook. Once a relationship is started, however, many people have a tendency to play a role. The society in which we live provides these roles—mother, father, child, friend, mister and mistress. Some people are more comfortable playing the role of mother/child or father/child than that of man and woman.

Consider a female child who was receptive to her father: a male might find it easier to relate to her by acting in a fatherly manner. The more he consciously or unconsciously takes on the father role, the more receptive she may be to him. In fact she is most likely to attract those men who find it natural to assume such a role.

A male child may have been particularly sensitive to an aunt. A woman relating to him might best reach him by unconsciously assuming the same role. He would also attract the kind of female who would feel most comfortable in this role. Or sometimes a brother or sister may have been a predominant figure in childhood. This would create a matrix in the unconscious which the individual would seek to fulfill in a relationship.

There is an interplay between the conscious and unconscious which eventually proves to be the essence of what an individual gives and receives in a relationship. Past life karma and early childhood memories form the basis for the unconscious, while the desire to improve one's life by creating a better future comes from the activities of the conscious mind. The unconscious is the ruler of one's past. The conscious mind seeks the experience of the present. If we are too entrenched in the unconscious, we may not be aware of all that a relationship has to offer. Similarly, if we are overly intent on being conscious without recognizing the existence of the unconscious, we may never be able to go beyond acting out the unconscious motivation in life. It is important for both mind levels to integrate, for as we recognize and cooperate with both we can seek and achieve a total relationship.

Spiritual Growth

All relationships contain potential for spiritual growth. Whether or not karma is involved, amidst the myriad subtle roles and identity interchanges, there is opportunity for each person to experience a spiritual relationship. The stream of each life may take many turns but it is always flowing. In some places the water is deep; in others, shallow. Sometimes the water is murky; sometimes its clearness is like the depths of pure soul itself. The water thinks not of what it can gain or lose as it nourishes the soil; it is simply there.

If we can learn to nourish another rather than clinging only to ourselves, even the most difficult aspects symbolized in a horoscope become part of the ever-flowing stream of life. We can ride on karma instead of being sunk under it. The burdens, responsibilities and obstacles that we cope with can eventually become the support which strengthens our ever-growing character. As the river of life changes direction, so does the raft of karma; never fighting the current, but flowing with it towards its eternal destination.

RELATIONSHIP ASPECTS

Relationships are the result of the ways in which individuals flow. There are no parents or children, husbands or wives, relatives or friends. We are all teachers and students—sharing, giving and learning as we flow through the stream of life. The superimposed roles often hide the essence of a relationship. If we can see these roles and realize the reasons for their existence, we can unfold the meaning and reason for any given relationship.

The aspects formed between two natal charts show the ways in which people learn from each other, as each helps the other to understand their karmic lessons.* As we go through life we are walking through an endless learning experience. Every time our unconscious is working something out, it calls into our lives the people who have within the pieces of the answer we are seeking. It is no surprise to find an endless stream of Arians coming into one's life for months at a time. Then, almost as suddenly as it started, the Aries people disappear, to be followed by a string of people born under another sign. This is the manifestation of what the unconscious calls for.

*See, *Karmic Astrology Vols. I-IV,* by Martin Schulman, Samuel Weiser, Inc., York Beach, ME, (1975-1979).

When an actual relationship or marriage is formed, the lessons to be learned are bigger ones and require a much longer time period and with more intimate contact. There are usually many lessons on many levels. The duality of the mind is brought to harmony through controversy. Mixed feelings are confronted, and as a result, each individual grows more in touch with himself. Questions of spiritual significance, opinions about one's place in the world, the battles that take place in the ego, all surface. Sexuality is understood on deeper levels. The totality of one's being is put to the test of how much it can expand and grow while retaining a modicum of harmony with itself, and the universe through which it sees its reference points.

We should understand that evolution occurs through friction. Criticism, altercations, differences of opinions and ideas are the catalysts. The essence of harmony does not mean the blissful ideal that we may imagine to exist in the "perfect" relationship. Bliss is not growth. It comes in moments as the result of struggle. Harmony can exist with the friction needed for unfoldment, for people can disagree with each other and yet their different ideas can be void of hate. People can criticize each other and still feel an overall harmonious flow on greater levels which override momentary corrections.

Conflict is often the source of enlightenment, yet too much conflict will violate harmony. When we look at the ways in which planetary positions in one chart affect positions in another, we must find the fine dividing line between friction and the differences necessary for growth, and the kinds of conflict that can ultimately destroy a compatible relationship.

It is important to realize that the biological, psychological, and sociological makeup of the female is different from the male. Astrological aspects can have one meaning for one sex and an entirely different meaning for the other. In the aspect interpretations in this book, care should be taken to read which planet is in the male chart and which planet is in the female chart. The astrologer never makes a final decision as to whether or not a relationship is workable. This is always the choice of the individuals involved. It is more important to point out the ways in which a relationship will contribute to the harmonious unfoldment of each person as well as the ways in which it can be destructive. The synthesis will show a strong leaning in one direction or another. Yet the question of whether a relationship or marriage should or should not be started or continued can really only be answered if one asks oneself the question, "What role does this relationship play in the cosmic plan?" Does it help the individual on his path? Does it make him more in tune with his place in nature? Is it ecologically disruptive to the grand plan in which each person is playing an important part? Sometimes we have to experience relationships that seem incompatible because there is something important to learn. On deeper levels there may be compatibility because we need growth within the Self and harmony with the universal intention. When we can see this, what might ordinarily appear to be a disruptive aspect might be interpreted as the weed killer without which the garden of love could not grow. The stereotyped "bad aspects" don't detract from one's sense of well-being. Instead they symbolize challenges and tests so that we can grow in harmony with ourselves and our universal purpose when we live through the experience.

Orb of Influence

The traditional 8-9 degree orb of influence allowed for natal aspects takes on a different meaning when we are comparing two separate charts. As individuals interact with each other, they soon discover that the greater the distance between two planets aspecting each other, the more difficult it is to communicate. Conversely, when planets are forming very close aspects (within 1-2 degree orb of each other) the effect is felt so strongly that individual identities often interchange as lessons are communicated on subtle, unconscious levels. Knowing this, we can look for close aspects to show us the intense transformations that occur in relationships, under-standing that although the wider aspect also has an effect, it is often less significant.

Aspect Strength

The major aspects (conjunction, opposition, square and trine) represent different degrees of intensity. The conjunction is the strongest aspect. Its effects are powerfully felt even if the orb is greater than one to two degrees, but when it appears within this orb the karmic interchange between the two individuals is so strong that it forces each person to focus his attention on the meaning of the aspect.

The opposition is the second strongest aspect. The pull from the opposite polarity forces each individual to understand the energy opposing his sense of direction and purpose.

Squares, which are next in strength, cause the necessary tension for growth because they generate movement and activity. Trines, which are the weakest of the aspects, bring a harmony that balances a relationship because each individual has energies which complement the other.

The closeness of the aspect, along with the kind of aspect it is, helps determine the relative strength it has and shows the exact nature of each inter-relationship tie. A conjunction five degrees from an exact conjunction will undoubtedly be felt more strongly than a trine with a four degree orb. A five degree orb on a square will be weaker than a six degree orb involved in an opposition. To help determine the strength of any aspect, it's important to consider the closeness of orb, as well as the relative strength of the kind of aspect in relation to other major aspects.

ASPECTS
TO THE INNER PLANETS

Sun Aspects

Sun Conjunct Sun. This aspect creates a natural warmth and an affinity for a similar perspective in life. There is a strong tendency towards competitive action which can bring out the best in both individuals. Because the two birthdays are either the same day or within a day of each other there is some difficulty in achieving a balance in the relationship. The subjective experiences of both may be so similar that one is either depressed or elated at the same time the other is. Other planets in the charts should be considered to see if the subjective energy will be balanced elsewhere in the relationship.

Male Sun Conjunct Female Moon. This is an excellent combination for bringing out the natural brilliance in the male for the female is receptive to him. The relationship will be male-dominated, yet the woman can fulfill a protective mothering role. This aspect brings vision and understanding to a partnership along with the more traditional promises of marriage. The relationship has creativity mixed with feeling—the two necessary requisites for a complete experience.

Female Sun Conjunct Male Moon. This aspect symbolizes a female dominated relationship. Although a natural affinity exists between both individuals, the male ultimately becomes the receptive follower. This kind of basis for a relationship can manifest different forms of resentment, through experiences which lack spiritual light. If the male can accept his role as the reflector of the female's light and power, this aspect can prove to be the foundation for a naturally compatible union.

Male Sun Conjunct Female Mercury. This aspect increases mental awareness and creates a relationship based on good communication. The female partner is valued for her ability to express ideas rather than for her femininity. As the Sun is the center of the solar system, the male is the center of this relationship; the female will find her ideas easily accepted and encouraged because of the hope and optimism coming from her partner.

Female Sun Conjunct Male Mercury. This aspect creates a strongly female dominated relationship. The male may feel threatened because he fears being reduced to a childlike role. He can learn a great deal from the female for she values him not for his sexuality, but for his mental potential. She will encourage him with her warmth and optimism as she helps him to develop his mind.

Male Sun Conjunct Female Venus. This aspect indicates natural warmth and consideration in a relationship. On unconscious levels a familiar caring, much like the interchange between father and daughter, will take place. Great material and spiritual wealth can emerge. The brilliance of the Sun and the love symbolized by Venus cojoin to create a sense of harmony.

Female Sun Conjunct Male Venus. This aspect appears in relationships where the male may have been "feminized" in a past life. Now he must draw his masculine strength and power from a strong female. The relationship will center around her. Because of her radiance and support, his creativity is brought out. The female will keep generating more strength because her unconscious animus figure will be brought to light through the male.

Male Sun Conjunct Female Mars. This signifies an active and progressive relationship. The female may draw power from the male and take action in her life because of her partner's influence. There may be some competition between them but this energy can be transformed through a common interest in sports and assertive activities. Sexuality can be heightened as the female is drawn to becoming physically and emotionally competitive with her partner.

Female Sun Conjunct Male Mars. With this aspect, the male tries to impress his mate because he feels her sense of power and pride as an obstacle to be overcome. Aggressive sexuality can take place, and the drive towards activity, accomplishment and progress will be heightened. Two flames burn as one.

Male Sun Conjunct Female Jupiter. Great abundance or a scattering of energy may be the result of this aspect, for it enhances and expands the experiences of both individuals. The male is centered while the female seeks freedom. Amidst the positive energy here, there can be some frustration on the part of the male. He thinks he must hold fast to his space. The female feels both an urge to run away as well as great magnetism for her partner. They can choose to pursue great wealth, or invest time in higher learning with this placement.

Female Sun Conjunct Male Jupiter. This beneficial aspect fills a relationship with hope and optimism. Both individuals feel a sense of freedom and enjoy sharing with each other. Both honor and wisdom are cojoined with a healthy competitive spirit that adds liveliness to the relationship. This is a powerful growth aspect which can lead to material riches and spiritual wealth. The coin shines on both sides.

Male Sun Conjunct Female Saturn. This aspect creates a sober relationship based on the soundness of feminine judgment. The exuberant and robust attitudes of the male are curbed by the mature wisdom of his mate. She garners a sense of purpose through the male. There is role playing here for the female tends to unconsciously project her image of her father onto her mate. As a result, she fulfills the karma of teaching him how to develop a strong sense of security within himself. The strength and power in this aspect can help a relationship endure through the most difficult setbacks as the female's sense of values and judgment (from the past) is added to all her mate stands for in the present. The male, like a nested eagle, proudly surveys his domain. His mate provides the fortress which will sustain his power.

Female Sun Conjunct Male Saturn. Here the male provides his mate with age and wisdom. He adds propriety, dignity and social tradition to her lifestyle. As a result, the relationship ultimately comes to stand for something greater than the two individuals involved. As the male fulfills the karma of strengthening his partner, she begins to understand her potential. This is a strong bond for marriage as it strengthens over the years. The female is as a blossoming flower, while the male protects her through her season.

Male Sun Conjunct Female Uranus. With this aspect, a vivacious liveliness colors the relationship. Hectic and undeveloped ideas spring forth from the female which causes the male to center in his own strength. Many changes, surprises and unexpected events will occur. A constant state of nervousness or sparkling electricity may be the norm. Relationships of this sort symbolize the conflict between the traditional and the bizarre. Although there is much excitement, the relationship lacks the stability necessary for endurance unless the partners are really mature.

Female Sun Conjunct Male Uranus. Here, the female who is trying to be herself must confront the male who is trying to change her. She sees him as being irresponsibly exciting and is attracted to his unconventional manner. When will and power are joined, there must be a sense of direction, for both forces need a common goal. Without this, the relationship may be active, but fragile; in many ways it may resemble the momentary brightness of an amusement park on the fourth of July.

Male Sun Conjunct Female Neptune. The pride and strength of the male, combining with the subtle subterfuges on the part of the female make this relationship intriguing but difficult. The Sun and Neptune symbolize Light and Love, the divine forces necessary for spiritual attainment. In this relationship both individuals must be caring and sensitive to each other. If they are, their union will be like a sparkling stream of impressions glistening in the morning light. If not, the relationship takes on the characteristics of dense clouds hiding the Sun.

Female Sun Conjunct Male Neptune. Here the male charms the female. Through his gentle compassion and sense of sacrifice he is able to bring out her artistic sensitivities. There may be a tendency for the male to be evasive as he attempts to find some vague or mystical sense of power. If both partners have realistic goals, the intuitive communication and the mutual receptivity to non-verbal communication will bring them close together. The male understands his mate in a similar manner to the way that water receives the Sun that warms it.

Male Sun Conjunct Female Pluto. This aspect produces the possibility for a volatile relationship. The darkness or unconscious drives in the female combine with the light of the male to create passionate extremes. The best and worst of everything are experienced. The male may transform the female through his light and she brings him to the depths he never knew existed. A fountain of truth springs forth from a well.

Female Sun Conjunct Male Pluto. This can sometimes be an exploitative relationship, because the male may try to find value in his partner that he cannot find in himself. At the same time, the female is trying to transform the male by giving him her light. Usually, she suffers as he brings her into contact with forces that she may be unprepared for. If the relationship continues, she will grow stronger and may ultimately learn how to find the depths within herself that the male has exposed to her. Only after experiencing what appears to be an eclipse at noon, does the female begin to understand the reason for the mystical depths she has experienced.

Sun Square Sun. This is an extremely difficult aspect. Both individuals strive to achieve a sense of self, but because their paths in life are different, some kind of struggle will take place. Life together causes a treadmill effect, putting frustration and obstacles in the way of progress. Yet obstacles are the stepping stones of strength. If the female realizes that being able to identify with her own femininity is secondary to identifying with her full self, then the difficulties here can be changed into a balanced optimism which leads to mutual self-respect and new awareness. Two lights each wait for their turn to shine.

Male Sun Square Female Moon. This aspect causes difficulties between the partners as they struggle to achieve their instinctual identities. Both may want the same goal, but because of past conditioning, each has a different idea of how to get there. The male must overcome unconscious memories of his mother; the female must stop being submissive to her unconscious conception of her father. If this is accomplished the relationship can work to the benefit of both partners.

Female Sun Square Male Moon. This aspect causes difficulty in perception and insight. Points of view, feelings and principles are often misunderstood as each individual is fighting an inner battle which has to do with sexual expression. The female may doubt her femininity and the male may doubt his masculinity. This personal problem will color the relationship, blocking even more important objectives, until each individual learns to overcome the anima/animus role reversals through which they are testing the other.

Male Sun Square Female Mercury. Here the male sees the female as a challenge. He may wish to influence the development of her femininity and sexuality. She may respond to him on a more platonic level or as a father image. The tension caused by the mental interchange of ideas produces much growth, but the tenderness needed in male-female relationships may have difficulty finding expression.

Female Sun Square Male Mercury. This aspect works well in platonic relationships because the female may view her mate unconsciously as somewhat of a brother figure. In either marriage or enduring sexual relationships the expectations of the male may not be met by the female. Tensions can manifest that are difficult to express, causing a lack of emotional fulfillment which results in frustration. Yet in a work or platonic relationship, this aspect can bring about the multitude of interesting ideas and work energy, even though the intrinsic harmony necessary for compatible achievement is strained.

Male Sun Square Female Venus. This is one of the most frustrating aspects in astrology. It causes sexual attraction and each individual expects to find what he is looking for in the other. But the relationship seems to fall short of its goal. The female may have some tragic flaw that makes her vulnerable; the male may be lacking the self knowledge needed to express the potential that the female sees in him. As a result, this aspect can be a source of inner frustration to both individuals.

Female Sun Square Male Venus. This aspect indicates a tendency for the male and female roles to be reversed on unconscious levels. The female often tries to find herself through the male energy expressed by her mate, yet she does not truly see him as a man. Conversely, the male sees all that he aspires to be in his female partner but he is not aware of her femininity. Instead, he feels the feminine side of himself which could be termed an anima projection. The female could be struggling through a past conflict with her father. The male keeps seeking his masculine role. Unless the two personalities are mature enough to have worked through these difficulties in previous relationships, the combination can stalemate.

Male Sun Square Female Mars. This aspect causes strong differences that make a relationship almost impossible. The male feels his masculine force being projected at him instead of emanating from him, while the female may be desperately searching for her femininity. A strong sexual force might be present in the relationship but because of its doubly positive polarity neither partner fully understands how to balance this energy.

Female Sun Square Male Mars. This indicates impulsiveness in a daring relationship. A youthful quality in the male sparks the female's sense of vibrancy. She must use her position of authority and power (that is, the masculine side of herself) to confront the charging onslaught of her aggressive knight in shining armor! Even though there are romantic overtones in the relationship, they are usually secondary to the ego battles through which each individual is testing assertiveness.

Male Sun Square Female Jupiter. This aspect causes basic differences in ideology which become more important later in the relationship than at the beginning. Value struggles because of differences regarding truth, honor, dignity, religion or education cause the personal autonomy which becomes the focal point for altercations. The independence of each individual is stressed.

Female Sun Square Male Jupiter. This aspect causes a pervading tone of self-righteous autonomy which makes it difficult for each partner to reach the other. There is a sense of philosophical distance in the male which causes the female to feel that her basic personality is not as important in the relationship as it should be. As a result, each individual experiences the frustration of not being able to reach the other. The relationship may indicate amusement and excitement but little real coming together takes place on the level where two minds and hearts meet.

Male Sun Square Female Saturn. This aspect creates a difficult karmic relationship. The male is symbolically striving to overcome the restrictions of his father. He unconsciously has chosen this relationship because he's questioning the value of transcending his heredity. He may wonder if he can cope with the guilt involved in doing so. He may see the female in a father role for she symbolically represents the limitations, traditions, and boundaries which he is driven to surmount. She may see the manner in which she imprisons herself in the relationship. The male gives her hope and optimism but she must also cope with a strong mundane reality. There are many hidden challenges here, as both partners can be highly conscious of achievement. Through struggle, each tries to enhance and maintain the dignity of the other. The male may eventually outgrow his mate, but if he does so, he must also help her build a sense of dignity.

Female Sun Square Male Saturn. In this difficult karmic aspect, the female may unconsciously attempt to outshine her father, the expectations of her family, or the traditions which have established her life. She can see the male as a symbolic limiting authority figure that she must transcend if she is to find herself. He, in turn, tries to keep the relationship anchored in reality and responsibility. Challenges and frustrations are caused by the female feeling cheated from experiencing her full recognition. As a result, there may be limitations and obstacles which can only be overcome when she realizes the full power of her Self. She must preserve the dignity and respect of the male (even if his ideas are contrary to her own) before she can fully understand her own power.

Male Sun Square Female Uranus. With this aspect, the male has to re-evaluate his conception of "woman" for the female refuses to yield to his direction. She may believe she can better help him because of her different approach to life yet the pride symbolized by the Sun makes it difficult for him to accept her unorthodox behavior, for he would rather see the female in a more "normal" feminine role. Her unpredictability is interpreted as a threat to him for he is often unable to control her or her sexuality. In spite of these difficulties, this aspect is excellent for growth because achievement can take place through progressive ideas, but it does lack the responsive yielding necessary for an enduring partnership.

Female Sun Square Male Uranus. This aspect causes frustration. The female sees the male as a contradiction to himself and feels that he does not really appreciate her warmth. The relationship can take many direction changes, often unpredictably and for no apparent reason. The spark present at the beginning of the relationship often generates an expectation of over-exhilaration, too much excitement and anxiety as time goes by. The female partner ultimately realizes that the male she picked lacks the soundness she is seeking.

Male Sun Square Female Neptune. This aspect can bring romance, but also may impede the forming quality that is a major goal in enduring relationships. The male has difficulty understanding his partner's psychic wavelength, for she tends to stray to different "psychic places." This causes difficulty regarding communication on inner levels. As a result, the male is forever seeking the female—but never quite reaching her. What appears to be a constant courtship situation eventually leads to the male realizing that he consistently winds up empty-handed. If the relationship is to work, the female must understand that she cannot continue to delude him.

Female Sun Square Male Neptune. Here we find deception built into the relationship. The female may have overly idealistic expectations which the male cannot meet. Often the attraction is based on physical appearance alone and the dreams that the image stirs in the female's unconscious. When reality rears its head, she may find the male is not a dream at all, but instead a very real person whose image may not be consistent with his real self. This aspect tends to encourage the male to lean on his partner for faith, inspiration, hope or the realistic attainment of his dreams. The basic difficulty is caused when he seeks his own reality through his mate; and she expects him to be the reality upon which her dreams can be built. This kind of relationship causes disillusionment.

Male Sun Square Female Pluto. This aspect tends to intensify unconscious paranoia in regard to the opposite sex. The attraction is so powerful that the female feels it at her very depths and tends to retreat into herself for protection. Both individuals fear being too open with each other, too exposed—

overly vulnerable. Both may have an almost obsessive interest in the other while seeking a distance that symbolizes safety.

Female Sun Square Male Pluto. This aspect can bring about in-depth insights that may first tend to cause misunderstandings. Each individual has to respond to new channels within before the other can be perceived correctly. The female may be viewed as a chaste virgin of light by her lover. He in turn is seen as the power that can overcome her virginity. She trusts him, but he may not trust himself. When the light and dark forces interchange, a great power emerges that can help the relationship flourish. First, each must deal with a personal conception of self.

Sun Trine Sun. Here a spirit of cooperation and harmony enables each partner to experience a sense of ease and optimism. Luck, fortune, material and spiritual wealth are possible as the life path of each individual provides complimentary opportunities for the other. Two lights brighten each other's pathways.

Male Sun Trine Female Moon. Here we find cooperation without competitiveness. True companionship can manifest on many levels as each individual has the necessary ingredients to balance the other. Parental residue in unconscious memories that enter into the relationship add color, flavor, a sense of direction and meaning to what can be an excellent partnership.

Female Sun Trine Male Moon. This aspect enables the female to express herself easily. She tends to lead the relationship, but the male finds it too easy to cooperate. He relies on her for advice, trusts her wisdom, and sees her as the light in which he can reflect. At the same time, while taking on the role of his mother, he discovers unseen blessings in his family.

Male Sun Trine Female Mercury. Here a tone of understanding and mutual interest is a keynote in the relationship. The male is able to share his partner's ideas, and she is capable of explaining his purpose. A mutual cooperation colors activities. Sometimes the female is highly respected for her capacity to understand this relationship. There may be a platonic note to this aspect which indicates a focus on the female's mental agility. She can be an asset because she helps the male understand his energy.

Female Sun Trine Male Mercury. This is an excellent aspect for cooperative activities that are both stimulating and fulfilling to both partners. Each is capable of self-reflection since their questions find answers in the other. Companionship is heightened because the need for understanding enables each to listen to the other.

Male Sun Trine Female Venus. This brings a sense of ease into the relationship but can cause some laziness as each partner experiences a sense of contentment in the other. Wealth, both material and spiritual, may manifest, because the relationship is cooperatively-oriented. The male is protective and able to assume burdens; the female is pliable and able to yield to her Apollo.

Female Sun Trine Male Venus. This aspect tends to take friction out of a relationship, thereby increasing harmony. Without friction there is little impetus to grow. These individuals may lack challenge. In this instance, the relationship is female-oriented and the male plays a cooperative but rather peripheral role to the unconscious mating of the woman with her father. She feels protected from within. He feels relieved of the burdens assumed by those who play the full "male" role.

Male Sun Trine Female Mars. Activity, achievement and a general sense of movement are at the core of this aspect. The relationship is male-oriented as the female tends to unconsciously identify with her animus figure. At the same time, the male finds her spirit of cooperation as an asset to his ego expression. Pride and accomplishment, along with the ability to master challenges easily lends a note of happiness to this partnership.

Female Sun Trine Male Mars. This is an excellent aspect for marriage. The youthful drive of the male cooperatively expresses the desires of the female. She warms and encourages him and gives faith and hope to his intentions. A comfortable level of sexual attraction is present. Goals can be striven toward with ease.

Male Sun Trine Female Jupiter. This aspect indicates compatible philosophies and a generally cooperative outlook on life. Both partners feel that truth and understanding are important. The female feels proud of her relationship and that feeling increases her desire to give love. This aspect enhances the luck, fortune, and brightness of the partnership.

Female Sun Trine Male Jupiter. This aspect brings wisdom and foresight into a relationship. There is an interest in expansion and travel. Because of the male's bounding spirit, the female feels that her potential for life is being fulfilled. He can lead his partner using truth and a kind of guidance that engenders a mutual respect and trust. There is an element of chance or unpredictability attached to this aspect and it may lead to gambling, scattering (particularly of investments), and a basic need for personal freedom. Ultimately, these interests can work positively as factors which create an expansive relationship.

Male Sun Trine Female Saturn. This aspect brings about a sober relationship. The female, through assuming a sense of wisdom and protectiveness will help the male to realize his potential. Goals, ideals, the ability to build on traditions from the past become important. The relationship is male centered as the female tends to unconsciously attribute to her mate the same sound judgment and wisdom that she attained from her father.

Female Sun Trine Male Saturn. This aspects brings a great deal of focus towards enhancing the status of both individuals. There may be a need to find some "correct" level in life. The female functions optimistically within the parameters set down by the male and this partnership functions easily within guidelines and limitations spelled out by both partners. If this relationship results in marriage, great wealth may be amassed later in life.

Male Sun Trine Female Uranus. Here the male is fascinated by the multi-faceted kinds of experiences to which he gets exposed because of his contact with this woman. She provides all the excitement he needs in his life. He becomes her source of inspiration. The relationship can be interesting and progressive; both partners can change and grow in cooperation with each other. The female is forever luring the male through her sense of detachment which serves as a never-ending puzzle for him to solve.

Female Sun Trine Male Uranus. Here the female is excited by the male's adaptability to change, for his endless array of experiences confront the relationship. She sees him as an unreachable ideal; as a result, he keeps gaining more confidence in his ability to transcend the traditional mores of society. This aspect requires the woman to be strong and secure in herself if the relationship is to be lasting.

Male Sun Trine Female Neptune. Here the forces of love and light combine in a gentle sensuous blend that is comfortable and soothing for both partners. Much warmth, artistic creativity, and even silent understanding between them can take place. The male is in love with a dream and the female imagines herself to be part of that dream. The light from the male illuminates her fantasies and builds his ego. The partnership includes the silent sharing which is the essence of harmony.

Female Sun Trine Male Neptune. Here the male is fulfilling the dream images of the female. His charm intrigues her; his unattainable quality mystifies her and challenges the power of her Sun to shine in its greatest brilliance. The more she tries to understand her mate, the more she grows in touch with herself. The male sees some of his dreams take form because of the stable and centered reality of his female. This aspect adds a note of glamour and idealization to a relationship.

Male Sun Trine Female Pluto. Here the forces of light and darkness blend to develop a sense of cooperative power which helps both partners to experience the best of two worlds. The male brings out crude energy in the female which helps her to become conscious of her strength. As she polishes her natural talents and develops strength she lifts her partner to greater heights. Many transformations occur through this aspect. The truth and light in the male can use the raw energy symbolized by Pluto to make its discoveries. The unconscious energy in the female needs to be mined and faceted before it can glow as the diamond it will eventually become.

Female Sun Trine Male Pluto. With this aspect a constant regeneration similar to the sexual force is surfaced and brought to consciousness. The female recognizes the raw qualities in the male as being necessary for her transformation. As the male unconsciously tries to control the light of the female, he inadvertently brings himself to truth. Great wisdom, wealth and power can occur through this aspect, with both individuals ultimately coming to realize a greater being within themselves.

Male Sun Opposite Female Moon. This aspect emphasizes a need to work through parental problems. The male acts out the difficulties he had with his mother while the female acts out the difficulties she encountered with her father. Because of this interaction, each can help the other to grow and mature. In the process friction may occur! Each partner is forced to confront the anima (in the male) and the animus (in the female) figures. A reworking of the unconscious expectations regarding these figures takes place. This aspect is difficult in a marriage for the natural harmony needed in a relationship is overshadowed by a need to work free of early childhood impressions.

Female Sun Opposite Male Moon. This aspect brings out childhood memories of the male's relationship with his mother. The female tends to dominate the relationship while the male unwillingly begins to get a new view of his childhood. The female may feel that she is burdened with a dual role—lover and wife, as well as mother. She may not like the role. This aspect is particularly difficult for marriage.

Male Sun Opposite Female Mercury. This is a particularly frustrating aspect for the female as she feels her femininity is misunderstood and her personal ideas are much different than her partner's. Communication may be thwarted for the male is unconsciously relating to a "male child" rather than a woman. This aspect is difficult for any relationship and especially difficult for marriage.

Female Sun Opposite Male Mercury. Here the female often possesses pride, stature, and significance while the male behaves in a childish manner although he may be unconsciously doing so. The male may feel threatened and insignificant; these feelings force him to confront strengths within that he may otherwise ignore. The female waits for him to express what she already knows he will say. Her superiority is enhanced because he strives to catch up with her. This aspect is not advisable for long-term relationships but it can be beneficial to both individuals over a short period of time.

Male Sun Opposite Female Venus. This aspect gives an attraction as well as indicating stagnation of the natural flow of love to light. Although the female is attracted to the male, her concept of love runs contrary to what he is able to give. He must either stop being himself in order to be what she needs, or he will learn to accept the distance that neither of them really wants. Both partners may attain great wealth between them but the actual manifestation will only be achieved with labor. However, unconscious laziness may impede their progress.

Female Sun Opposite Male Venus. This aspect tests both partners in their role identities. The female, to be herself, must often go against her natural love instincts, while the male, attracted to her strength, has a tendency to give in to the "male will" he sees in her. He admires her, yet experiences a lack of fulfillment in himself.

Male Sun Opposite Female Mars. This is a quarrelsome aspect. The female is more aggressive than the male expects she will be, and there is too much competition between them in the relationship. Each person grows more independent as a result of knowing the other. The individuals may experience a growing apart from each other rather than coming closer together.

Female Sun Opposite Male Mars. Competition, exuberance and a battle of the egos take place with this aspect. The male ego strives for supremacy while the female is often upset. Sexuality may lack the tenderness indicative of real caring and may be more a manifestation of unconscious desires aimed at overcoming challenges rather than displaying love. The relationship tends to display an inherent wildness that makes marriage or an enduring partnership extremely difficult.

Male Sun Opposite Female Jupiter. This aspect indicates differences in basic life philosophies. Each individual tends to remain individualistic without developing the full sense of sharing that adds warmth to a relationship. There may be a lot of travel or great wealth involved, yet the female can lose some of her femininity and perhaps her sex drive as she feels forced to compete for recognition from her mate. This is a very difficult aspect for marriage.

Female Sun Opposite Male Jupiter. This aspect adds an element of chance to a relationship and scatters feelings of security. While both individuals maintain a sense of individual freedom, the female often provides the security for both. A basic lack of communication and understanding makes the two lifestyles pull in opposite directions. Each partner will eventually re-evaluate principles and philosophies if the relationship is to work.

Male Sun Opposite Female Saturn. This aspect causes heavy responsibilities for the female partner. In her effort to cope she may lean on memories of her father whose lifestyle was different from her mate's. Struggle, strife and eventually a strengthening of her inner spiritual being must take place. The male feels his life becoming more responsible because of the seriousness he perceives in his partner. Although difficult, this relationship can endure as each learns the karmic lessons of strength, patience, and sound judgment.

Female Sun Opposite Male Saturn. This aspect produces a "bondage" situation and the female's brightness may be all but squelched by the overprotective or overbearing attitudes of her partner. He may see himself as a wise man when he's with her, secretly feeling more youthful because of her but not revealing these feelings for fear of losing his authoritative role. The relationship can last if the female doesn't have a strong need to completely express the Sun of her personality.

Male Sun Opposite Female Uranus. This is one of the most difficult aspects for a relationship. Eventually the male sees the female as being insensitive, while she tries to assert her free will. Sexual attraction is erratic and sometimes non-existent. The male may feel the burden of the relationship is on him. Although he has warm feelings towards his mate, he might be relieved if the relationship ended.

Female Sun Opposite Male Uranus. The female is proud of the unconventional inventiveness of her mate. He depends upon her security and may see her as his anchor, his reality, his audience, his promoter, even his center of being. Yet, through a clashing of wills, he may unconsciously deprive her of the closeness she needs. Through his interchange, the female learns to become more independent, while her mate is forced to learn to understand the value of warmth, tradition, and responsibility. At best, this aspect is difficult for an enduring relationship.

Male Sun Opposite Female Neptune. This aspect engenders a basic lack of trust on the part of the male. Although he is intrigued by the female, he cannot really trust what he cannot fathom. Sensual and sexual attraction are often strong, but the male feels he is losing himself in some gossamer mist that is unexplainable.

Female Sun Opposite Male Neptune. This aspect makes it difficult for the female to trust her mate. Promises may be denounced before he can even get to keep them! Intrigue, charm, mystical longing are included in the relationship, but the female feels she must fight to maintain her sense of sound judgment.

Male Sun Opposite Female Pluto. This aspect is difficult for enduring relationships. It tends to create a strong sexual attraction but a great deal of distance separates the two individuals. There may be a tendency for the male to degrade the female, as though revealing her most sordid past will help him find the most honorable parts of himself. The battle between the forces of light and darkness becomes a constant source of irritation. Even so, this tie can result in a great deal of growth as both partners try to understand if night follows day or day follows night.

Female Sun Opposite Male Pluto. This aspect tends to create an arena for animal instincts to surface. The female's honor is literally ravaged by the crudeness of the male as he moves from the lowest depths within himself to get in touch with her light. In time, she may grow spiritually strong, as he begins to realize that there are higher levels to Plutonian energy. Sexual degeneracy sometimes appears with this aspect, yet if the female has high moralistic ideals she will be fortified against it. If the female acquiesces at the beginning of this relationship, she will ultimately rise above it as her sense of honor and self-respect become stronger through testing.

Moon Aspects

Moon Conjunct Moon. This aspect indicates instant intuitive understanding. Both individuals know each other's moods, emotional shifts and needs. As a result a strong sense of emotional compatibility and insight develops, through a creative and emotional flow which enhances the relationship.

Male Moon Conjunct Female Mercury. This is an interesting aspect because the partners' emotions are understood rationally and communicated easily. The male may feel a certain amount of frustration when his feeling responses are met by the cold analytical mind of his partner for he may expect or want warmth and emotion. He will eventually learn that her attitude helps balance any over-reactions he retains from childhood. At the same time, the female learns how to be more feminine as she emulates her mate. Unconscious role reversals of both male and female ultimately can be corrected because each will learn about himself from the other.

Female Moon Conjunct Male Mercury. This is an excellent aspect for compatibility. Both the feeling and thinking aspects of life meet and balance. The female may be particularly attracted to her mate for she can sense his every thought. This may cause the male to feel overly "mothered" but, on the whole, he tends to enjoy her receptivity to his analytical mind.

Male Moon Conjunct Female Venus. This aspect causes a "feminine-oriented" relationship. Artistic interests, musical taste, and the developing of personal talent are areas of importance. However, the female must be responsible if the partnership is to work. Although her mate is sensitive, she cannot lean on him any more than she can lean on her own inner emotional experience.

Female Moon Conjunct Male Venus. Emotions and feelings are joined to form a very special sensitivity between the partners. The male shows the more gentle side of himself and by doing so allows the female to express her more vulnerable feelings. Many childhood memories, especially those of the teenage years, may be acted out in this relationship. Wealth, an accumulation of property and possessions may result from the instinctive harmony and sharing that comes out of this partnership.

Male Moon Conjunct Female Mars. This is an impulsive aspect. It brings out the instinctive and the progressive sides of both personalities. The energy can create a strong sexual attraction and the female may be the aggressive partner. Youthful activities and responses produce a lively relationship. There may be an Oedipal conflict released from childhood as each partner copes with the role reversals expressed by the aspect. The female responds as if she were the male relating to childhood images of his mother. The male may unconsciously respond as if he is the mother of his mate as he attempts to balance his feelings with the more primitive qualities of her ego. Each can become an important teacher for the other.

Female Moon Conjunct Male Mars. The feminine mystique responds to the male sexuality and acts as the background for its expression. There is a strong sexual attraction and a magnetic possessiveness that help hold the relationship together. Still, impulsiveness must be curbed if the partnership is to endure. Spontaneity and progressive hopefulness for the future combine with action to eventually conquer the challenges of both egos.

Male Moon Conjunct Female Jupiter. Here the female is able to lift the male to a higher consciousness. It is practically all but impossible for him to experience depression in her presence. His emotions expand as the female learns how he responds to her ideas, as she helps him to see the higher truth in all he feels. This aspect tends to decrease sexuality as it emphasizes the female's higher mind. However, the increased awareness, the optimism and joy symbolized by this aspect allow the relationship to express a fulfilling sense of happiness.

Female Moon Conjunct Male Jupiter. This aspect frees the female from past inhibitions and repressions because her partner brings out feelings of exuberance and abounding freedom. The relationship brings opportunity and luck into her life, while the natural hesitancy she may feel helps hold the male's interest. Sexuality is less important with this aspect, but the joining of her feelings with his expansiveness make a perfect combination for an enduring partnership.

Male Moon Conjunct Female Saturn. This aspect binds a relationship, solidifying its intention and bringing the two individuals together because of karmic experiences.* The male feels the causes while the female must be responsible for the results. Because she is aware of the outcome of things, she tends to inhibit her mate, forcing him into a lifestyle that is traditional and responsible. As a result, he may feel somewhat caged, but also finds it difficult to break his possessive attachment to the female. On unconscious levels, the male takes on the role of his mother while the female plays out the lifestyle of her father. As a result, the relationship grows deeply rooted in customs, values, memories and unresolved karma from the past.

Female Moon Conjunct Male Saturn. Here each partner acts out a parental role. She plays mommy, he plays daddy—each trying to emulate the original family. A possessiveness pervades the relationship, along with a sense of reserved wisdom and sobriety. The male tries to impress his sense of dignity. She needs to mature, for her emotions are patterned in a childlike manner. This relationship is karmic and often depicts residue from a marriage in a former incarnation. In many instances there are religious or spiritual lessons that the female must learn from the male.

Male Moon Conjunct Female Uranus. This aspect brings excitement and instant attraction! An enduring relationship is

*See *Karmic Astrology Vols. I-IV,* by Martin Schulman, Samuel Weiser, Inc., York Beach, ME, (1975-1979).

difficult for the partners may be too unpredictable. Expectations can be unfulfilled or the two way flow of love that makes a partnership complete doesn't seem to be present. The male seems possessive and dependent upon his more aloof and detached partner. She either leads the relationship because of her willfulness or ends it because of her need for spontaneity and freedom. Emotional development and awareness are both possible if these people are mature enough to recognize each other's differences.

Female Moon Conjunct Male Uranus. This aspect creates a very interesting relationship. The female tends to live in the past while the male is carving out the future. Instant sexual attraction is heightened but actual sexuality may lack security or fulfillment. She is involved emotionally but her individualistic mate seems unable to provide her with the sense of safety and comfort that she seeks. Despite this, personal growth and evolution of spirit can take place in this partnership.

Male Moon Conjunct Female Pluto. This aspect symbolizes a direct psychic link between two individuals. It causes powerful magnetism and strong sexual attraction. But the relationship is actually much deeper than that. The unconscious needs of each partner surface because of the other. The female shows the male the conscious cosmic meaning of the collective unconscious so he can grow out of a form of emotional isolation. This dynamic and forceful partnership may also engender great wealth.

Female Moon Conjunct Male Pluto. A psychic link between both individuals brings a great depth to the relationship. The female depends upon the male for he can show her the hidden cosmic truths symbolized in her emotional reactions. The male can break through the sham connected to old memories to help her energize great transformations. The sexual attraction is strong, and the intense passion may keep these two together long enough to discover other important facets in personality and relationships.

Moon Square Moon. Each individual sees the tensions caused by past experience as a threat to the present relationship. The mothering influence within both partners is expressed in different ways so conflicts may take place. Sexual attraction may be high but the differences of opinion in regard to matters of family, home, children and feelings may cool the romance.

Male Moon Square Female Mercury. The male unconsciously acts out his childhood difficulties. This time, however, he may take on the mother's role while his partner acts as he did during his elementary school years. She in turn may see him as similar to her own mother whom she may not have agreed with. The difficulty caused by this square will depend upon the friction experienced by each individual during the childhood years. The female must intellectually sever the umbilical cord with her own mother, since the male (in the role of his mother) symbolically fights to preserve his nest.

Female Moon Square Male Mercury. This aspect causes tension between the female's natural mothering instinct and the male's ability to relate to her. There may be blocks in communication which hinder the flow of the relationship. The female does not feel the male "force" she may seek and may turn inward or stop relating if she unconsciously feels some threat to her femininity.

Male Moon Square Female Venus. This aspect indicates tension. The female may be forced to confront an unconscious rivalry with her mother, while the male may consider the female as a source of tension between himself and his own mother. Because this is a female dominated relationship, the male often feels thwarted in his attempts to successfully achieve the masculine role he wants to play. As a result, this aspect brings out inner struggles in both partners that cause difficulty when attempting to relate honestly.

Female Moon Square Male Venus. Here the female tries to play her mother's role, yet she sees the mature maternal instinct fighting the child. Because of never fully resolving her childhood relationship with her mother, she tends to transfer this role to her partner. As he struggles for his own sense of worth, he in turn re-experiences conflict with his own mother and the inner feelings of resentment he may have had. As both individuals carry feelings from the past, those feelings have to be resolved if this relationship is to last.

Male Moon Square Female Mars. Here the male unconsciously battles himself as he allows the female to act out most of his ego desires that contradict all he was taught by his mother. His partner may feel he is pushing her away. She may also have difficulty understanding her own aggressive tendencies in this relationship, for she is unconsciously battling with her own mother through her mate. As a result, she may try to make him seem inferior as she attempts to develop a stronger sense of herself. Sexual attraction is present but sex may be used as the unconscious battleground where the child attempts to extricate itself from the parent.

Female Moon Square Male Mars. This aspect can cause a high degree of sexual tension. Since Mars symbolizes the youthful male and the Moon represents mother, there may be some unconscious incestual temptation hidden in this relationship. The female receives her "God of War" but cannot really be herself in the process because in some vague or unconscious way she may feel she is violating an acceptable role in society that she wants. Thus, she tries to convince herself that she is not overwhelming her mate, while he in turn keeps striving for dominance. The partnership can be fraught with tension and unconscious apprehension.

Male Moon Square Female Jupiter. This aspect causes exaggerated feelings resulting in unsound judgment. The male's possessiveness clashes with the female's urge for freedom. Still, the optimism with which she is able to lift the male's consciousness comes from her basic free spirit. Thus, there is an irreconcilable conflict here which can only be resolved if the man raises his level of consciousness.

Female Moon Square Male Jupiter. Here the basic protective instincts of the female are thwarted for her knight in shining armor is quite capable of protecting himself. He rejects her emotional responses in favor of his power projections. Unable to express the basic instincts her mother taught, she may unconsciously retreat back into a more childlike state rather than facing her inability (as a woman) to take the wildness in the man she loves.

Male Moon Square Female Saturn. Here the male may act the role similar to that of his mother as she attempted to achieve recognition from his father. The female partner feels tension from her parental influence. She may unconsciously play a role similar to that of her father when he vainly attempted to impress some kind of social dignity upon the mother. This relationship contains built in feelings of fear, bondage, and the continuance of karmic stress from past generations.

Female Moon Square Male Saturn. Here each individual plays a parental role. An extension of each family and family values comes to conflict through this partnership. For karmic reasons, the male tries to dominate his partner in some kind of traditional manner. The female feels blocked because the male is not really receptive to her emotional responses. The more she represses her feelings, the more the male feels his dominion over her is valid. If this relationship is to last, there has to be an open reappraisal of personal values.

Male Moon Square Female Uranus. Possessiveness in the male is heightened for he is unconsciously jealous of the whimsical "female attitudes" that constantly frustrate his need for emotional security. He feels threatened by a universal sense of freedom expressed by his partner. He may wonder why he cannot agree with her more liberal attitudes. In reality, she is attempting to free herself from her mother; she rebels against her partner when he looks for mothering. This is a poor aspect for an enduring partnership.

Female Moon Square Male Uranus. Here the female experiences emotional frustration as the male is both dependent upon her for security while trying to keep himself free from emotional bondage. He sees her as his symbolic mother and views the relationship as the challenge he must overcome to assert his own individuality while he struggles to sever the unconscious umbilical cord. She finds him exciting, stimulating and unique, but she can never truly call him her own, for part of his attractiveness comes from the impractical flights of fancy and changing curiosities which are forever loosening him from emotional entanglement. This is an extremely difficult aspect to build a lasting relationship on.

Male Moon Square Female Neptune. This aspect brings confusion into the relationship. The male senses an escapist attitude in the female but he can't really define it. He may try to provide protection and security but he's never sure of her loyalties or intentions. Thus, a sense of deception tends to cloud the basic issues. The male unconsciously tries to please his mother, while holding onto the woman of his dreams. In reality he experiences a feeling of failure, yet if he searches for mystical answers he only furthers his sense of loneliness and frustration. Inevitably, he may symbolically become Don Quixote chasing windmills.

Female Moon Square Male Neptune. The female experiences a sense of unconscious loneliness, for her idealized concept of relationships keeps dissolving. The more she tries to identify with her mate, the more she loses herself. He may try to find himself through her mothering instinct, while unconsciously resenting the re-enactment of a symbolic childhood from which he is trying to escape. A great deal of psychic interplay takes place here as each person reaches for the other on many levels. Misunderstandings and a lack of clearly defined goals as well as identity confusion make it difficult for both individuals to define the partnership.

Male Moon Square Female Pluto. This aspect tends to bring power plays into the relationship. On a psychic level, each individual is confronting and testing the other. The female tends to be destructive to the male's conception of family security. The male in turn may view her as all that he could be if he were more assertive. Sexual intensity runs high, but so does competition and jealousy. The symbolic protective male instinct meets its match in the female who can really protect herself!

Female Moon Square Male Pluto. Here the female is literally thrust into Dante's inferno. The relationship forces her to break away from her past but she is not promised a secure future. The male is trying to break away from the womb. He may try to symbolically degrade his mate in order to feel his own power. The struggle takes place between the dark side of the male which needs to surface and the female who can only reflect the negativeness of her partner. Eventually, if each person faces the struggle within, a relationship can work out.

Moon Trine Moon. The emotional quality of this relationship is harmonious. Both individuals understand each other's feelings without losing themselves in the process. Companionship, cooperation, and a spirit of helpfulness make this an excellent combination for an enduring partnership or marriage.

Male Moon Trine Female Mercury. The male likes the relationship because he finds the understanding that he sought from his mother. He feels secure expressing his emotions and enjoys the way in which the female is able to focus his unconscious feelings. She in turn enjoys his receptivity to her ideas for his response helps her develop harmony with herself. There may be a childlike quality to the relationship. The male may feel threatened but his fears are easily overcome because the female perceives his feelings.

Female Moon Trine Male Mercury. This aspect indicates easy communication. The female symbolically displays passion and the male combines emotion with reason so that each partner functions in the most harmonious archetypal way. The male enjoys the mothering quality of his mate, while his logical mind provides a secure foundation for her feelings.

Male Moon Trine Female Venus. In this female oriented aspect both mutual sensitivity and receptiveness take place. The male finds the fulfillment of his needs. She complements the pattern of love he learned from his mother. Thus, the love he receives from his mate is familiar to his unconscious. This aspect adds a note of ease to what can be an excellent relationship.

Female Moon Trine Male Venus. This is an excellent aspect for enduring compatibility. The female feels emotionally comfortable and her mate enjoys her comfort and mothering instincts. Creativity is increased for both as the Divine Mother principle feeds the relationship from the natural resources of the universe. As a result, a steady flow of feelings, intuition, and cooperation keeps building the harmony of the partnership. The male is able to appreciate the way his mother has been instrumental in nourishing his needs. Thus, it is easy for him to transfer mother love to his mate in a positive way.

Male Moon Trine Female Mars. The aggressiveness of the female acts as an impetus to all that the male needs to express. By showing her mate his emotional nature, she learns how her own mother's emotions can be combined with action to achieve progressive goals. Ultimately she transfers her image of her mother to herself and provides the male with the fullness he is seeking. The relationship is lively and active.

Female Moon Trine Male Mars. The female's natural mothering instinct combines with her mate's desires as he leads her onward to the future. The attraction is instinctual and comfortable to handle. The female learns how to put her instincts into action while the male learns how to act through instinct. A lively cooperative spirit pushes this combination to new discoveries—about themselves as well as their relationship to the world. Yet, if this partnership is to last, both individuals have to curb an often restless or even reckless attitude.

Male Moon Trine Female Jupiter. This aspect adds a note of happiness and lightness to the relationship. Expanded feelings teach the male how to find his place in the universe. The female learns how the emotions combine with her higher mind. If the couple is careful about excess, this aspect can create a strong emotional truth center in the partnership. When excess is not curbed, however, an emotional "looseness" may affect the security of the relationship.

Female Moon Trine Male Jupiter. The two individuals experience harmony in travel, philosophy and finding their station in life. The female values the free spirit of the male and provides a comfortable nest for him while he helps develop her emotional self and expands her consciousness. This aspect does not bind a relationship, but can add enjoyment to a partnership if it is otherwise sound and stable.

Male Moon Trine Female Saturn. This aspect brings a sense of sobriety and caution into a relationship. A reserve binds the two individuals together in ways which may isolate them from the rest of the world, yet neither individual feels as if he is in bondage. The male welcomes the female's projections of her father for they add to his maturity. She in turn is proud of the ways in which he grows to assume the role of dignity that she needs. As a result, this aspect can produce enough stability for an enduring partnership or marriage.

Female Moon Trine Male Saturn. This aspect creates a harmonious balance between the female's emotions and the male's need for stature. Both individuals feel protective towards each other. The female's ability to yield to the male for his strength and wisdom makes this relationship compatible. She recreates the role of her mother as she tries to fulfill traditions from the past; the male imposes the traditions that make her feel that she is part of something larger than herself.

Male Moon Trine Female Uranus. This aspect adds excitement and exhilaration to a relationship. A note of unpredictability keeps each individual interested in the other. Through her sparkling originality, the female teaches the male how to relate more flexibly to his emotions. He in turn provides the emotional stability so she can safely express her individuality. While this aspect does not bind an otherwise shaky relationship, it does add the potential for insight through which both partners can grow.

Female Moon Trine Male Uranus. Here the female unconsciously takes on the role her mother played in an effort to help the male free himself from his ties to his mother. His sense of freedom helps him establish his unique identity and the female is able to understand this without losing her own sense of self. The combination of original expression and inventiveness in the male and harmonious receptivity in the female can make this a very interesting relationship.

Male Moon Trine Female Neptune. This aspect indicates an unconscious receptivity in both individuals. Each understands the other's feelings on intuitive levels and a gentle romantic flow guides the relationship. Like a woman bathing in moonlight, the partnership reflects one of the most harmonious combinations of nature. The male warms the female with affection as she soothingly sings for his efforts. Her inspiration helps him birth his eternal feelings for the universe.

Female Moon Trine Male Neptune. Here the female sees the idealized dream of herself in the male. Like rain on fertile soil he pours his love on her and she grows to the image of his ideal. There is mutual intrigue and psychic understanding for both partners as their creative imaginations move towards the same vantage point. Like Cyrano De Bergerac, the male compassionately woos his waiting Roxanne.

Male Moon Trine Female Pluto. This aspect brings depth and insight to a relationship. The male nourishes the female by reaching into the well of her unconscious so that she can transcend her lower self. She in time can become the diamond he is patiently searching for. He must understand her volatile nature and how much it is asking for transformation. Through deep caring and sincere love, both individuals can literally transform each other.

Female Moon Trine Male Pluto. Through this psychic aspect, the female tries to transform her partner. She reaches through the thorns to find the tiny seed that will ultimately bring about his birth in consciousness. If he lets her lift him, through the passion and pain the transformation of darkness into light can take place. The great challenge in this aspect can product a partnership that is of lasting social significance.

Moon Opposite Moon. This is a difficult placement for compatibility as the emotional responsiveness of the two individuals is opposed to each other. There is great attraction and both aim at achieving a balanced sense of objectivity. But as each person tries to center himself, emotions may be taken to extremes. This causes intensity and passion which adds excitement to the relationship. Ultimately, however, this intensity may cause the relationship to end.

Male Moon Opposite Female Mercury. This aspect indicates that the male's feelings may be contradictory to his partner's ideas. Her analytical outlook regarding his emotions may make it difficult for a meeting of the mind and heart to take place. Frustration and discontent may ultimately disrupt the partnership.

Female Moon Opposite Male Mercury. A natural opposition between thought and feeling causes friction. The female's mothering instinct opposes the male's ability to think for himself. His ideas tend to be different than the patterns of feeling and behavior to which she is accustomed. As a result, unconscious childlike expressions of resentment may disturb the harmony of this relationship. In general, there may be a lack of understanding on both parts which never really allows a smooth communicative flow.

Male Moon Opposite Female Venus. This aspect causes difficulties on feeling levels. The relationship tends to be female-oriented. The female unconsciously battles through her competitive instincts to survive under her own mother. The male, often with a difficult childhood, is drawn to this relationship in order to develop new emotional attitudes. He unconsciously sees the re-enactment of his own mother's preoccupation with her womanhood so that he can learn the lessons which put him more in touch with his true feelings.

Female Moon Opposite Male Venus. Here the female sees herself as her mother and herself being expressed by the male. She may feel threatened and may create situations so her man will chastise her. Through his force she can learn to differentiate her own feelings from those projected on her during childhood. This presents a difficult psychological complex which can truly undermine a relationship. The male tends to be rather peripheral to this entire complex and he may become resentful. Both individuals may never see each other for what they truly are. Working through this complex may be beneficial but the solution to the problem may ultimately end the relationship.

Male Moon Opposite Female Mars. This aspect tends to bring rash or impulsive action into a relationship. The female acts out the male role. The male sees himself as the female while he unconsciously plays the role of his mother in opposition to himself. In order to win freedom from the mother influence he must create situations in which the argumentative female (played by himself) wins. The more he does this, the more he extricates himself from his past. Still, the present relationship suffers as this problem is being worked out.

Female Moon Opposite Male Mars. Here the male unconsciously relates to his mother through the female. The strong sexual attraction indicated by this aspect thus carries hidden incestual undercurrents that inhibit this relationship. At the same time, the female tends to unwillingly act out her own mother's unconscious feelings. There may be a great deal of friction, passion and conflict in both partners.

Male Moon Opposite Female Jupiter. Here conflict exists between the male's possessiveness and the female's free-spirit. He attempts to communicate his emotional feelings and expects her to do the same. She relates to him through her higher mind instead. As a result, the relationship is really functioning on two different levels of consciousness that may not complement each other. This conflict manifests as strong differences of opinion, opposing philosophies, and conflicts in attitude that are difficult to resolve.

Female Moon Opposite Male Jupiter. Here the female's natural instinct towards motherhood is thwarted by the male's need for freedom. She senses an irresponsibility in him that leaves her feeling unprotected. He believes she is over-reacting to his need for expansion, abundance and tasting all that life has to offer him. Thus, he often fails to offer her enough security so she can display some vulnerability. The bright optimism she feels leaves her despairing during moments of true confrontation.

Male Moon Opposite Female Saturn. This aspect places a dour tone on a relationship. Both individuals tend to act out parental conflicts which disturb their personal sense of harmony. This occurs because the female has unconsciously absorbed some guilt from her father and tends to project it onto her partner. He feels restricted for reasons that have little to do with his present situation. Karmic patterns are unwoven here, as the female's difficulty in understanding male emotions must be overcome if the relationship is to work.

Female Moon Opposite Male Saturn. This aspect often causes a bondage situation in which the female fights for her emotional freedom and the male expends a great deal of energy attempting to dominate her. Confusion between the anima figure in the male and the very real female he is confronting makes true communication difficult. The male tries to impose his sense of wisdom, dignity and propriety on the female, and she feels overwhelmed. Relationships with this aspect can last for an indeterminate period of time until each individual reaches some kind of karmic maturity.

Male Moon Opposite Female Uranus. Here the unpredictable behavior of the female brings out past insecurities in the male. She is symbolically rebelling against the protectiveness of the womb. Erratic patterns stem from her latter teenage or college years when she began to experience her own originality and independence. By unconsciously seeing the male as a surrogate mother figure from whom she must free herself, she is unprepared to give to the relationship all that she could. This aspect is extremely difficult and too unstable for marriage or an enduring partnership.

Female Moon Opposite Male Uranus. Here the male sees the female as symbolically representing the values held by his own mother in the past. He feels a need to rebel against any form of domination and may strive to assert his sense of freedom and originality. The relationship will not be dull, but the female is in for a surprise ending if she becomes dependent upon the male's erratic nature.

Male Moon Opposite Female Neptune. This aspect causes feelings of loss in the male. He reaches for the female only to find she is not there. Instead, he confronts dreams, illusions, fantasies and battles with Maya, when in fact it is the sensitivity to his very real feelings that he seeks. In turn, the female's animus image doesn't agree with what she sees in the male. She becomes confused, and may try to make him fit her ideal, thus creating a dream she will have to live in. Because of the difficulties caused by this aspect, the relationship can easily turn into despair.

Female Moon Opposite Male Neptune. This aspect makes it difficult for both individuals to express true feelings to each other. The male may hide behind images which mask his real identity, while the female keeps trying to surface feelings in him that she assumes are there. She is reaching for the wind as it constantly eludes her grasp. As a result she may grow disappointed in herself or tend to lose her sense of identity.

Male Moon Opposite Female Pluto. This brings a volatile, explosive quality into a relationship. The female keeps recharging the male, yet he sees her force as a threat to his sense of security. Arguments leading to breaks, separation and endings ultimately bring the male to a more cosmic understanding of his feelings. The female, in turn, tends to destroy the very home she is seeking as she pursues a constant need for regeneration.

Female Moon Opposite Male Pluto. Here the regenerative force of Pluto is often too much for delicate feminine emotions. She may feel threatened by the dark side of life, not understanding the depths she is being lead to. The male seeks to personify "Male" through her responsiveness, but may find her too staid to fulfill his energetic drive. The energy is symbolized in the classic case of Diana's confrontation with Lucifer as the Moon Goddess tempts the Devil. In mythology she wins, but in reality there is no winner for the aspect challenges the very essence of both individuals.

Mercury Aspects

Mercury Conjunct Mercury. The two individuals think in a similar manner. An unconscious re-enactment of sibling competition may take place if either partner had to compete for attention with a brother or sister, yet the expressive needs of both partners ultimately can create a situation of clear-mindedness and innocent understanding. They are very much like two children playing under the protection of a universe that cares. Through their ideas and perceptions of each other they can grow closer to share reason, logic, and a spontaneous comprehension of each other.

Male Mercury Conjunct Female Venus. Here the reasoning ability of the male complements the kind and cooperative spirit of the female. She is in love with his mind. He in turn stimulates feelings in her which warm his neutral logic. The simplicity created by this aspect stimulates easy communication and emotional expression. The messenger speaks to his love who patiently waits to hear his message.

Female Mercury Conjunct Male Venus. She likes him and he enjoys talking and sharing with her. A childlike ease makes this aspect comfortable for both partners. A sharing of common interest, along with an appreciation for the arts acts as a common bond of understanding.

Male Mercury Conjunct Female Mars. This male-oriented aspect indicates that she energizes his intellect. She may be frustrated, for her sex drive is lifted to a mental plane because the male misinterprets what he perceives. Still, the relationship is active, lively, and competitively stimulating. It helps to negate any escapist qualities that might be indicated in other areas of the chart comparison.

Female Mercury Conjunct Male Mars. The male projects his sexual force, but she uses the energy as a stimulant to express her ideas. Subsequently, he feels thwarted because his sexual instincts are misunderstood, but grateful that his needs are comprehended on other levels. This aspect forces the female to use her mind in healthy competition with the male ego. Thought is joined with action. Reason and progress may be the ultimate goal of this partnership.

Male Mercury Conjunct Female Jupiter. This aspect indicates a meeting of the lower and higher levels of the mind. The male helps bring the female's expansive ideas into practical reality while she can show him a higher consciousness. In essence, he is the funnel her consciousness pours through. Because of his ability to categorize and understand, her sense of worth as a cosmic being is enhanced.

Female Mercury Conjunct Male Jupiter. Here the female finds her higher mind through the male. He explains the universal intention of her subjective consciousness, and helps her to see a more elevated attitude towards life. A humane quality pervades as the female's thirst for knowledge and understanding feeds the male's need to give from his cup of wisdom.

Male Mercury Conjunct Female Saturn. The female leads the male to his lessons. She talks to him about responsibilities, burdens, and the means for attaining wisdom that will add fullness to his being. He needs to earn her respect and as a result strives to develop stature. The more flippant qualities of Mercury are impeded as she impresses the wisdom of mature consciousness on the childlike qualities she sees in her male.

Female Mercury Conjunct Male Saturn. The female finds the support and protection that she expects in the male. A reasonable attitude gives purpose and direction to the relationship. She asks questions and gets serious answers in morals, proverbs, quotations; serious responses that help her develop security. The aspect symbolizes the child looking in the father's eye saying; "Daddy teach me?", and he does.

Male Mercury Conjunct Female Uranus. Here the intellect of the male blends with the unique originality and inventiveness of the female. It forms an aspect of interest and powerful mental stimulation. Through her ability to think freely she can show her partner the exciting possibilities of his mind. At the same time, his ability to perceive and understand her ideas adds a note of practicality and reason to a relationship which can exude genius.

Female Mercury Conjunct Male Uranus. This aspect heightens intellectual stimulation. The female is able to understand the erratic thought processes of her mate. Although his ideas may make her feel scattered, she ultimately realizes there is more to life than what she knew before. Expressive originality adds excitement to the partnership which can grow by leaps and bounds as it constantly transcends the conventional archetypes and norms of more common partnerships.

Male Mercury Conjunct Female Neptune. Here the male reasoning ability combines with the inspiration and vision of the female. The male shares his practical ideas and helps her understand her vision. She is able to soothe him as he pursues the reasons for all her impressions, fantasies, and deeply psychic feelings. However, she may lose her identity as she melts into her partner's mind, as her sacrificial and compassionate nature yields her entire being in order to introduce her mate to the deep mysteries she feels within.

Female Mercury Conjunct Male Neptune. This aspect symbolizes a blend between reason and intuition as the male helps the female find belief in her ideas. He has vision and inspiration. She has the ability to analyze and understand. The relationship symbolizes the message on the waters of spirit as the female thinks her ideas and is then shown the divine inspiration in them. A sense of compassion can make this an excellent aspect for a partnership if the male understands all that Neptune has to give.

Male Mercury Conjunct Female Pluto. Here the conscious mind of the male confronts the raw unconscious energy in the female. This may be a relationship built on alert perception and depth. She shows him the ultimate extension of his thoughts, while his interest in learning is fed because of her inceasing transformations. If the male tries to dominate the relationship he may feel as though he is sitting on a volcano which might erupt at any time. Yet if he understands how intense his partner is, then he can appreciate his slow introduction to knowing the unknown.

Female Mercury Conjunct Male Pluto. This is an excellent union for spiritual growth. The ever-transforming male creates upheavals which help change the female's ability to perceive herself. She begins to develop depth as she starts to overcome any narrowmindedness that might have otherwise stifled her lower mind. The male also changes her sexual ideas, and although she is frightened by his intensity, she is nevertheless intrigued by it. Thus he lures her deeper into the mysteries of the universe in search of understanding the core of life itself.

Mercury Square Mercury. This aspect causes irritation because both partners think differently and the challenge of expressing unique ideas causes friction. A dynamic quality in the relationship may create growth. Because this aspect causes repeated tension on mundane levels, it is especially poor for the establishment of harmony.

Male Mercury Square Female Venus. Here the male tries to mentally teach the female how to express her love. She may feel thwarted at the androgynous "Mercury-like" vibrations which present an intellectual rather than a "full-male" essence for her to relate to. The male may unconsciously tell her "Be as I say, not as I am." With this tension, even mundane communication becomes difficult.

Female Mercury Square Male Venus. The female questions her role as she confronts the feminine side of the male. While she questions the relationship (both from his point of view as well as her own), she is trying to accept the female role which is being shown to her. In essence she asks the male to teach her how to love, but through this aspect she can only understand love on her intellectual level.

Male Mercury Square Female Mars. This aspect causes disagreement, friction, and irritation. The female may be unconsciously identifying with her male animus figure, and as a result, she may attempt to overpower the intellectual part of herself she sees symbolized in the male. She may act or react instinctually, perceiving his thoughts as stimulants rather than a sharing of ideas. As a result, the male experiences a lack of communication in this relationship.

Female Mercury Square Male Mars. Here the female tries to understand the nature of the relationship and her role in it while the male is subjectively expressing his ego. She must perceive what he doesn't. To do this, she may play both roles hoping to gain understanding. When she attempts to play the male role, however, she not only antagonizes him, but also hurts herself. As a result, this aspect tends to disturb the harmony that both individuals are seeking in a relationship.

Male Mercury Square Female Jupiter. Here the male uses the female to expand his consciousness. She is able to explain his thoughts to him, but he may not like the explanations or they may not suit his path. Instead, he may feel scattered or doubt his original questions. She may have difficulty relating to the information he feels is meaningful. Both the higher mind of the female and the lower mind of the male do not complement each other, although they both may be valid.

Female Mercury Square Male Jupiter. This aspect causes communication difficulties that are not easily overcome. The female relies on the male for higher truth, but may find his conception of truth is not in line with hers. He may play the role of prophet, sage, or soothsayer in answer to the questions she poses. The answers cause her to see aspects of truth that are not really useful to the direction her thoughts are moving in. As a result, she must either change her point of view or resign herself to an inferior role in the relationship.

Male Mercury Square Female Saturn. Here the male uses his intellect to unconsciously challenge the traditional limitations and wisdom of his father that he sees symbolized in the female. To him she symbolizes purpose and slow movement towards productive goals. He may think this is a hindrance to free expression. If he listens to her, he will ultimately grow more thoughtful and learn how to say what he means and mean what he says. If he doesn't, then she may be burdened by the karmic effects of his ideas. The relationship can either be one-sided or extremely meaningful, depending upon how the male accepts her practical and sober outlook.

Female Mercury Square Male Saturn. The female unconsciously sees the male as symbolizing an overbearing father figure who suppresses her need for expression. She feels thwarted and frustrated as most of her ideas meet with obstacles. The male sees himself as responsible for her ideas. A very obvious superior-inferior relationship may develop where each person goes to great lengths to impress the other. This is a rather difficult aspect for harmony because of an undercurrent of bondage. Both may question their role in the relationship. The female can be afraid of the male, as he builds a sense of esteem on her fears. The more he delays the expression of her ideas, however, the stronger she gets, until one day she'll no longer need his overprotective instincts.

Male Mercury Square Female Uranus. This aspect produces a vivacious attraction on mental levels. There may be lots of excitement, but along with it goes a tendency for unexpected, disputed, or hectic experiences caused by the female's unconventional attitudes. The male looks to her for originality, inventiveness and a higher expression of his intellect. Instead her strange ideas may shock his thinking process. He seeks stability in his partner only to find she is forever changing.

Female Mercury Square Male Uranus. An active lively relationship is possible but there may be difficulties regarding communication. The female questions her mentality because the male expresses himself in such a unique and original manner. The more he seeks the existential life, the more he disrupts her attempts to understand mundane reality. She thinks he is a most exciting character, but every time she thinks she understands him he adds something new. She feels like she's looking through a kaleidoscope of possibilities that keep moving just beyond her reach.

Male Mercury Square Female Neptune. Here the active mentality of the male may be disillusioned by the female's mystique. At the same time, she may feel confined by his analytic attitudes. She may attempt to help him develop his intuition so he can feel what he's trying to understand through reason. As his reason grows increasingly less effective, however, he may see the female as a shadow over his thoughts. Mistrust or oblique communication makes this aspect difficult for the establishment of an enduring relationship.

Female Mercury Square Male Neptune. The female cannot find her image-ideal in the male. He is a dream, but she is never sure if he is her dream, or the illusive projections of what he knows she wants to perceive. Like the man of a thousand faces, he can be anything she thinks except the substance she truly needs. As a result, self-deception caused by this aspect can easily erode an otherwise sound relationship.

Male Mercury Square Female Pluto. This brings a quarrelsome and argumentative tone into a partnership. Fanatic competition for self-expression tends to emphasize the baser qualities in both individuals, yet each is capable of transforming the other. The male seeks to understand the depths in the female and though she may lead him through darkness, she promises light at the end of the tunnel. To do this, however, she must unconsciously learn to understand what he is trying to communicate. Effort, struggle and tension are involved as both partners attempt to understand each other.

Female Mercury Square Male Pluto. Here the female has difficulty seeing the hidden side of the male. She senses a "Trojan Horse" exterior and fears it may invade the order in her mind; however, she is intrigued by this deep dark mysterious force that seems to know all that she doesn't. As a result, she is both attracted and repelled at the same time. Thus, she must use her wits to deal with the volatile challenges of the male. The relationship is intense and passionately opinionated as each individual tries to communicate the importance of their thoughts to the other.

Mercury Trine Mercury. The conscious intellect in the male is compatible with the ideas and thoughts of the female. The two complement each other as friendly children walking side by side, sharing ideas together. This is an excellent aspect for mutual understanding.

Male Mercury Trine Female Venus. This aspect brings a sense of cooperation into a relationship. The female tries to understand the male and because she loves him, he gains confidence in his ideas. They appreciate the arts and share a common sense of constructive values. This is a positive aspect for a compatible partnership.

Female Mercury Trine Male Venus. This aspect brings a note of tranquil harmony into a relationship. Through cooperative understanding both female and male benefit from sharing their experiences. The female sees her sense of aesthetic appreciation in the male as he adds feeling and tone to her intellect. If she has a practical mind, this aspect can produce an excellent foundation for communication.

Male Mercury Trine Female Mars. The female energizes the male's intellect. She sparks his ideas and helps him develop confidence in his beliefs. At the same time he can add reason to her passion. The relationship is lively, active, and progressive as the youthful aspirations of both partners act as a propellent towards the future. The aspect is excellent for achievement. When the male doubts himself the female encourages him. She can boldly overcome obstacles while he can discriminatingly choose the most sensible path for them to follow.

Female Mercury Trine Male Mars. The female's intellect is powered by the male drive for expression. She sees the need for putting her thoughts into action and his energy helps her to do it. Active communication is directed towards mutual understanding as the partners can both help to build each other. Both can attain wealth and fulfillment of personal desires if a good amount of "uncommon sense" is incorporated into the relationship.

Male Mercury Trine Female Jupiter. Here the male's lower mind combines with the female's higher mind to create many levels of harmonious understanding. She may generously feed him ideas that he can assimilate intellectually. Thus, he experiences a comfortable expansion of his consciousness. At the same time he provides a vehicle for expression so she can communicate her ideas. If he is practical and sensible, this aspect can cause spiritual growth for both partners. When reason combines with light, the Renaissance begins.

Female Mercury Trine Male Jupiter. The female intellect is illuminated as it combines with the male's ability to understand the expansive nature of the universe. He introduces her to new ways of thinking, and she may be fascinated as she sees the value of expanding simple ideas. Once Jupiter lights her torch of reason, she becomes a messenger of truth able to give her enlightened understanding to others. Not only personal growth may be indicated by this aspect, but also the possibility for fulfilling a spiritual calling.

Male Mercury Trine Female Saturn. The female contributes maturity which acts as a buffer, protecting and focusing the male intellect so he can achieve meaningful expression. Her unconscious projections of purpose and sound achievement provide the nest from which the male's ideas are born, nourished, and strengthened until they can be brought to fruition. This is an excellent aspect for an enduring karmic partnership or marriage.

Female Mercury Trine Male Saturn. Here the male contributes his sense of purpose. He helps raise her outlook so she begins to have more mature thoughts. As a result, she becomes the avid pupil in a student-teacher relationship. Through a karmic blending of meaningful ideas, both individuals experience spiritual evolution. She learns that it takes time to build all good things, while he helps her build her consciousness.

Male Mercury Trine Female Uranus. This aspect brings about harmony between the male's intellect and the unusual or inventive knowledge that the female gleans from the world. Through his "lower" mind, the male seeks to categorize and analyze all he perceives. When he does this, he may overlook much that could enrich his thinking. Through his relationship with the female, he becomes more inventive, original, and more in touch with numerous existential possibilities that he might not have otherwise considered. A touch of genius can come out of this relationship, if both individuals work cooperatively towards the same purpose.

Female Mercury Trine Male Uranus. This aspect causes the male to freshen and renew the mind of the female, who is excited and exhilarated by his intelligence. She comes to recognize new potential, broader horizons, and may even begin to understand concepts never before possible. When the lower mind is enriched by the vivid discoveries of Uranus, an endless progressive tone is added to her intellectual capacity. She learns how to reach beyond her grasp for the brightness of an improved future. At the same time, the male finds her order and logic a welcome channel for his unconventional ideas, giving direction to energy that might be wasted.

Male Mercury Trine Female Neptune. Here the reasoning ability of the male gains insight and inspiration from the female. Her dreams complement his concrete reality. She may encourage him because her beliefs and visions can teach him how to perceive aesthetic natural beauty, as well as uplifting his intellectual ability. Appreciation of music and the arts adds to the compatible harmony of this aspect.

Female Mercury Trine Male Neptune. This aspect can teach the female to accept the mystical awareness she receives through the male. Instead of concluding her thoughts, she may begin to realize that keeping an open mind helps her to reach new levels in consciousness. As she wades into the spiritual realm that the male provides for her, she discovers many nuances, images, meanings, and colors that cosmically exist in what she expected to be simply a personal relationship. This is an excellent aspect for an evolving partnership or marriage.

Male Mercury Trine Female Pluto. This aspect brings great depth and wisdom into a relationship. Through the exploration of the source of ideas, the male learns how to transform his thinking. And, since a man is what he thinks, he can change his entire being. The female is the hidden "Angel of Light," mysteriously providing the secrets which hold the keys to his evolution. The relationship is powerful and dynamic as it churns its way towards harmony between conscious thought in the male and unconscious emanations in the female.

Female Mercury Trine Male Pluto. The female drinks deep from the well of passion and mystery as she fills her cup of understanding to the brim. What may appear to be excess in the male can cause the generating of power from the very depths of his soul, which will ultimately transform the consciousness of both partners. She is "Little Red Riding

Hood" who meets the Wolf, only to learn that the wolf is the catalyst that will force her to transcend her fears and self-doubts.

Mercury Opposite Mercury. With this aspect the conscious mind opposes itself as both partners see life through a dichotomy of opposites. The relationship may achieve a balance, but the individuals may never feel truly centered. Mental harmony results when you accept a universe of opposites. If each individual can truly acknowledge and recognize the validity of the other's thought streams, then this combination can bring both to an objective consciousness. If either of the partners is too personally attached to thoughts or opinions, this opposition can be a hindrance to communication and may make the partnership intolerable.

Male Mercury Opposite Female Venus. The male intellect works against his need for love. The female may feel confronted with ideas that irritate her sense of well-being. The more the female is stimulated by the thoughts of her partner, the less she may be able to express the feminine side of herself. There is a natural conflict between the female's need to give love and the male's intellectual reaction to her.

Female Mercury Opposite Male Venus. The female may not enjoy her mate's expression of love. She may see her female mystique expressed in the male, whose softness and kind nature may pose a threat to her sexuality. As a result, petty irritation tends to mask a larger and more meaningful conflict which may never really surface. The male tends to feel that he never really communicates with her to his satisfaction.

Male Mercury Opposite Female Mars. This is an argumentative aspect, and the female may struggle to overpower what she sees as male supremacy. She may identify with her unconscious animus figure and feel a need to win in the communication area. But every time she does, she loses more of her feminine nature, for she makes the male less confident in regard to self-expression. In essence, she seems to be condemning his ideas.

This is a particularly difficult placement for an enduring partnership or marriage, as communication includes a debasing quality. Both partners try to build on each other's weakness for the sake of survival.

Female Mercury Opposite Male Mars. The female's intellect may feel threatened by the aggressive force from the male. She is aware of his sexuality on a mental level, yet she may try to rationalize his aggressiveness or attribute it to other causes. As a result, she has difficulty communicating her feelings. A tinge of inferiority pervades her thought processes, provoking anger from her partner. He may wish her to be more submissive, feeling threatened sexually when she responds too intellectually. Nevertheless, this aspect can cause growth in the female and can lead the male to a complete re-evaluation of his need for self worth.

Male Mercury Opposite Female Jupiter. The lower mind of the male and the higher mind of the female conflict with each other. She is exuberant, but cannot relate to her feminine role without also coping with his lower mind. The relationship is a constant searching for identity transmuted to levels that never really confront the main issue. He sees her expansiveness as avoidance of the feminine role that he wants her to play. She may see him as unwilling to assume his masculine role or unwilling to communicate with her on the level she would like. And even if he did, their views would probably clash.

Female Mercury Opposite Male Jupiter. The female sees the mental freedom and agility in the male that she would like to reach in herself but cannot. As she analyzes his higher mind through her lower mind, she may try to elevate her lower mind function but she can't relate for long in this manner. He may constantly show her the insignificance of her ideas in comparison to how he perceives the universe. As a result an unconscious inferiority can become the focal point of this relationship, destroying what could otherwise be a mentally stimulating partnership.

Male Mercury Opposite Female Saturn. This aspect causes some role confusion on the part of the female if she is unable to accept her own hidden tendencies to either dominate or impose responsibilities on the male. She may secretly believe he is pushing burdens on her. In truth, she is perceiving the male through the expectations of her father, while he is perceiving her acting a role that does not truly fit her. He may also be unwilling to accept the demands put upon his otherwise agile and adaptable intellect. There may be struggle and strife as the male, in attempting to find his own significance, feels he must oppose any sense of responsibility that is not his own.

Female Mercury Opposite Male Saturn. Here the female must find a dispassionate strength within herself in order to overcome the weight of responsibility and traditional rules that she feels burdened by because of unconscious father images. She may not perceive the male as a person who knows what is good for her, for she feels that he restricts her thought patterns. Although this response causes difficulties in a relationship, this aspect can symbolize an enduring union. The female must break from the father figure, and her mate in turn must have patience with her. Both might unconsciously enjoy the struggle which ultimately makes each stronger.

Male Mercury Opposite Female Uranus. This aspect causes a battle of wits where each is trying to outguess the other. The ingenuous female fights for her liberal attitude while the male convinces himself that he understands her mind. In truth, her unpredictability is incomprehensible to his ordered intellect. A hectic state of sheer madness can prevail which make this relationship too unstable to last.

Female Mercury Opposite Male Uranus. Here the female is puzzled by the unique mind of the male because his ever-changing direction excites her intellectually, yet causes her to see her own inferiorities. She seeks order and finds chaos. She looks for logic but must confront all that eludes logic. Since her femininity is not a part of this aspect, she may find herself at a disadvantage. She must compete with the male on his ground, but when she does, she may discover that his erratic ideas or unconventional methods of expression prove to be a constant source of irritation. As a result, there is friction, misunderstanding, and in some instances, pure madness resulting from this aspect. When rebelliousness is opposed to reason, the discord can keep the relationship from being fruitful.

Male Mercury Opposite Female Neptune. This aspect can indicate that the female deceives the male. Rather than adding to his ideas, her sense of vagueness makes it difficult for him to think clearly. Here we find Plato symbolically representing reason, in opposition to the Water Nymph whose mystical charm can lure him from his sensibility. Knowing this, the male may attempt to protect himself by mistrusting his mate if he perceives her as the quicksand eroding his consciousness. This can be a testing aspect for the male's spiritual growth, for he must learn how to be clear-minded amidst the clouds of illusion that keep pulling on his senses.

Female Mercury Opposite Male Neptune. Here the female tries to understand the elusiveness of the male. He intrigues and mystifies her, while luring her childlike gullibility into his sea of illusion. She seeks knowledge upon which she can build a stable reality only to find herself confronting Peter Pan in Never-Never land. As a result, this becomes an extremely difficult aspect for a lasting relationship.

Male Mercury Opposite Female Pluto. This aspect causes conflict between the conscious awareness of the male and the unconscious depths of the female. He may feel that she can literally destroy his mind and may try to guard himself against any sinister tendencies he perceives in her. As she tries to express her power, he may resort to his wits in a contest that sees each battling for identity. The female can ultimately transform herself by learning how to perceive the lighter side of life, while the male can learn much about the depths he never knew existed. In the process there may be antagonism, friction, and so much conflict that neither is comfortable with the other.

Female Mercury Opposite Male Pluto. Here the female feels the eroding undertow of the male's unconscious depths that literally shake her from her roots. Nevertheless, she is intrigued by all he seems to know, as well as the ways in which he can deeply understand her. Transformations occur as the male keeps trying to get the female to change. She feels he is a burden and yet an inescapable confrontation that she must experience. The relationship carries a foreboding quality with it that forces each to their ultimate potential. Growth occurs but because of the disharmony, this partnership may be only short term. It may be too volatile and irritating for an enduring relationship or a marriage.

Venus Aspects*

Venus Conjunct Venus. This is one of the most beautiful aspects for an enduring and compatible relationship. Each individual has the same concept of love. As as result, there is natural agreement in the things that make up a relationship. A general air of kindness and a gentle understanding tend to pervade the relationship as both individuals are able to reflect their feelings through each other.

Male Venus Conjunct Female Mars. Here the individuals experience role reversals as each tends to unconsciously identify with their anima and animus figures. The male receives the female through the unconscious feminine part of himself. She in turn symbolizes the aggressiveness that she is looking for from him. There is an extremely magnetic and sexual attraction although the female is playing the lead role.

*See *Venus—The Gift of Love,* by Martin Schulman, Golden Light Press, West Palm Beach, Florida, 1981.

But through his love for her, the male inadvertently expresses his own narcissism, for he may be unconsciously drawn to the male ego projection coming from his partner.

Female Venus Conjunct Male Mars. This is one of the most naturally compatible aspects in the zodiac. Each individual is in the most comfortable role since Aphrodite symbolically soothes the aggressive Mars. Strong sexual attraction magnetizes the two creating a passionate and dynamic relationship. The male's sexual desires find an acceptable receptivity in the warm feelings of his partner.

Male Venus Conjunct Female Jupiter. This aspect brings a note of pleasant harmony into a relationship. The male's love nature is expanded because of the female's higher mind. At the same time, she can unconsciously see her own identity through him. Optimism, generosity, and an open feeling of nonbinding love pervade the relationship as sexuality becomes secondary to a more fulfilling experience. If both individuals are prudent, great wealth can occur through this aspect.

Female Venus Conjunct Male Jupiter. Here the female seeks the wisdom of a prophetic mate. His sense of knowledge and freedom can help her to expand her consciousness as well as brighten her outlook on life. He lights the torch which sparks her to encourage his endless search for truth. With a practical attitude and a realistic outlook on the part of both partners, this aspect can bring great fortune.

Male Venus Conjunct Female Saturn. Here we find a harmonious role reversal; for the male, unconsciously identifying with his anima figure, tries to please the partner's unconscious expectations of a father image. She, in turn, identifies with her father's protectiveness. Acting out her father image, she can add security, wisdom, and strength to the male. Growth occurs slowly but surely as genuine caring becomes the predominant keynote of this relationship.

Female Venus Conjunct Male Saturn. In this karmic aspect, the male takes on the role of his father and provides a secure foundation for the female whom he unconsciously sees as either a daughter or sister. Although at times she feels he is overbearing, she nevertheless can give him the close affection and fond admiration that his efforts deserve. Through mutual respect and sincere caring this aspect can form a permanent bond of love.

Male Venus Conjunct Female Uranus. This aspect can bring about an instantaneous attraction which may too powerful to endure. The male, unconsciously identifying with his anima figure, may respond to a free and independent spirit in the female that he wants to achieve in himself. He admires her originality and unconventional attitudes. She sees in him a feminine part of herself—one too delicate to express. As a result, each is learning about himself from the other. When love combines with electrifying changes, a heightened sense of magnetism prevails. However, even though each partner is enriched by the experience, the attraction may be too intense to form a lasting relationship.

Female Venus Conjunct Male Uranus. The female, in her role as Aphrodite, attracts the Uranian male. He becomes her enthusiasm, her vitality, and in essence her point of interest or understanding of what life can mean. He is able to free her natural love instinct. If she is overly possessive, he will rebel, yet if she understands the kind of impersonal love he needs, then she has much to contribute to the relationship. Each day can bring new discoveries about the original and inventive way through which love can blossom.

Male Venus Conjunct Female Neptune. In this female-oriented relationship, the love nature of the male blends with the compassionate giving nature of the female and creates an easy stream of consciousness through which the feelings of each for the other can flow. There can be both creative understanding and artistic appreciation as the positive characteristics of Venus find expression through Neptune's awareness of Divine Love. Both individuals are sensitive to each other's needs because an unconscious attunement helps their feelings flow.

Female Venus Conjunct Male Neptune. Here the musical and poetic qualities in the male are aroused because the female is receptive to his aesthetic senses. He can show her the limitless ocean of love in which her feelings swim. Aphrodite may be intrigued or fascinated by the waters of imagination that surround her form. She may see her dreams in a vaguely gossamer existence which eludes definition. The male softens the outside world for her and teaches her how to blend with nature. This is one of the most beautiful aspects for a memorable romantic involvement. It may, however, lack the practicality that one seeks in an enduring partnership or marriage.

Male Venus Conjunct Female Pluto. This aspect causes the male to identify with his anima while trying to transform himself. She may never let him know that she is, in fact, his "shadow," expressing the undercurrents of all he loves. The causes of her volatile reactions or intense passions are often hidden. Yet as time goes by, and intensity deepens, the love feelings bring about a mystical bond that seems to go to the very core of love itself. Changes and transformations of the male's conception of his role are at the center of this relationship.

Female Venus Conjunct Male Pluto. Here the female feels the depth of the male reaching for a response that she is unaccustomed to expressing. A passionate sexual attraction draws the two together and keeps regenerating movement and change. The past is forced away through each new discovery in the present. There is a secret quality to this love and it preserves the strength of its original essence. Few people experience these feelings for long periods, for this aspect causes love to be mystically regenerated. As the female finds herself, the male realizes his regenerative power and accepts his cosmic role into the Grand Plan. Even the lust—which this aspect often produces—is part of each person's acceptance of himself as being no more nor less than nature's offspring.

Venus Square Venus. Here the male feels the identification of the female and she sees another manifestation of femininity in him. On an unconscious level, he may experience a sense of failure because his efforts to relate to his partner make him appear to be trying too hard. As a result, this aspect is difficult for a lasting relationship. The male must learn how to retreat if he is to keep himself from being affectionately overbearing.

Male Venus Square Female Mars. Both the male and female experience role reversals, because by trying to reach the other they tend to play the role partner. In this way, unconscious needs are discovered. The male, as he tries to identify with his aggressive nature through the female must confront his own passivity. As he sees her attracted to his gentleness, he may have difficulty understanding that she is trying to reach her own femininity through him. Although this aspect causes sexual attraction, both partners must understand each other if the relationship is to last.

Female Venus Square Male Mars. Through powerful sexual magnetism, this aspect can create a passionate and intense relationship. The female's instincts bring out the raw id in the male. Because both may relate on base levels, there tends to be a lack of humane consideration. Each sees the possibility of fulfilling sexual passion but may not come in touch with the value of civilized decency. As a result, this partnership may lack the inner morals or standards necessary so that each individual can see the other as a full person.

Male Venus Square Female Jupiter. The male confronts the expansive nature of his mate. He may try to hold her mind with his love, yet her innate sense of freedom or a desire for an open consciousness may prove to be an irritation to his possessive nature. She can see herself in him, but cannot exude the femininity she is searching for. As a result, she may run from the love she wants or experience frustration at not feeling centered within herself. If she gives up her freedom, she may find female identification, but she may lose the independent knowledge which makes her a "person." Thus, this aspect creates a personal dilemma which makes a lasting relationship difficult.

Female Venus Square Male Jupiter. This aspect causes the female to experience feelings of insecurity. She waits to receive her love and may find that his expansive nature seeks more from life than a one-to-one relationship. When she tries to offer affection, his identification with philosophical attitudes, proverbs and distant ideas may be a constant source of irritation to her. Misunderstanding her intentions, he can try to impress her with knowledge or noble and chivalrous attitudes rather than giving her the love and affection she is looking for. If the male is willing to abdicate the throne of his understanding, then he can begin to feel all she is trying to tell him.

Male Venus Square Female Saturn. A karmic interplay of experiences can cause growth for both individuals. The male, unconsciously playing the female role, sees the overbearing attitudes of his father in his partner. Because she oppresses his aesthetic sensitivities, he symbolically relives the love feelings he gave to his own father; feelings which appeared to be received only with coldness. At the same time, the female may see herself taking on a fatherly role in order to help the male consciousness mature. She wants him to accept more responsibility rather than focusing his feelings only on the pursuit of beauty, nature, or the aesthetics. An unconscious frustration takes place as she senses these qualities in him. She would probably rather play a feminine role in the relationship, if only he would lead her with his strength. As a result, both individuals are experiencing karmic lessons that are difficult to learn. Irritation, frustration, a blockage of feelings, and a sense of bondage may be the prevailing factors that make this aspect seem like the legendary Gordian Knot.

Female Venus Square Male Saturn. Here the female works through any unconscious problems that she may not have yet resolved with her father. She may take on a daughter role and as a result may try to symbolically attain her father's expectations through her relationship with her mate. The male, rather than relating to her on an equal basis tends to see the inferior qualities that he wants to mold and change if she is to meet his Saturnian standards. The karma indicated by this aspect involves each learning how to see the other as an individual, regardless of the roles they both play while helping each other solve problems from the past. A strong sense of attachment creates a pseudo-family relationship. The aspect is extremely difficult, but is often necessary for those individuals who need this experience as part of their evolutionary path.

Male Venus Square Female Uranus. The aspect creates a spontaneous attraction which often results in an extremely hectic relationship. The male tries to hold the female by reflecting the feminine nature he may feel she seeks, while she fights for her psychic space. As a result the relationship has the quality of holding together and splitting asunder at the same time. Insecurities on both parts may be accentuated by the erratic and inconstant nature of this aspect. The relationship can easily take on the quality of a whirlwind blowing with no apparent purpose.

Female Venus Square Male Uranus. Here a powerful magnetic attraction creates a great deal of stimulation for a relationship. The female's instincts to warm, soothe, and perhaps even own the male are thwarted by his sense of individuality and independence. He sees her as one of his aspirations, but as he reaches out to her he may worry about his idealization of personal freedom. Thus, there is an almost impersonal sense of distant admiration on his part that he may not fully understand.

Male Venus Square Female Neptune. The male tries to find his dream through the feminine part of himself. Rather than seeing his mate as she truly is, however, he tends to see his collection of impressions and idealizations. At the same time, she can understand her feminine nature through knowing him, but cannot feel her feet on the ground when she perceives herself in the relationship. Although there is sensitivity, compassion, and gentleness in both individuals, tension is also caused by each never truly knowing their real identity. The partnership may lack the spark of intellect that could put much needed reason above feelings.

Female Venus Square Male Neptune. This aspect tends to add a depressive note to a relationship. The female tries to see all that she idealizes in the male. He intrigues her with the impressions of his personality that ultimately cloud or hide his real character. The more she is susceptible to his charm and mystery, the more she loses her own conception of "woman." Sensuality, teasing, and individual testing of magnetic powers can hide the real love that each is seeking. An element of doubt inherent in this aspect makes it difficult for the female to fully trust the male, even though she is constantly drawn into his magnetic mystique.

Male Venus Square Female Pluto. The gentle feminine love nature in this male may be challenged by the crude or unconscious impulses in his partner. She may pose a threat to his sense of security because she topples his values—those very things he believes can soften her feelings toward him. The more he responds to his anima figure, the more he feels degraded. Although this aspect increases sexual attraction, there is usually too much friction for the male to feel comfortable in the relationship. However, the female can transform herself through her partner, for she can learn to eliminate any raw or crude behavior while refining herself into a less volatile, but more effective, woman.

Female Venus Square Male Pluto. The female feels all that the male cannot see in himself. While he views her in her natural role, she sees many of the inner perceptions that affect his consciousness. Nevertheless, it may be extremely difficult for her to cope with the relationship because his intensity tends to throw her off balance. The more she tries to help the male transform, the more she is destroying pieces of her past. Spiritual growth can occur, yet the turmoil and upheavals which cause the growth may be too volatile for an enduring partnership or marriage.

Venus Trine Venus. This aspect helps to create an easy flow as both individuals experience compatible feelings and a harmonious interest in the aesthetic side of life. The male feels some identification with his anima but this, too, adds to the cooperative instinct in the female. If there are other compatible aspects, a sound partnership or marriage can emerge through a sense of decency and common morality.

Male Venus Trine Female Mars. This is one of the most interesting aspects that can occur in a relationship. The male experiences an unconscious identification with the female part of himself while the female unconsiously identifies with the male. In this case, the role reversals are harmonious, for each accepts the other. Sexual attraction may not be as strong as with the conjunction, opposition, or square. The more aggressive role is enacted by the female. Ultimately, the moderate tension from this aspect can bring about a much sturdier and long lasting relationship rather than the more volatile aspects which only produce a heightened sexuality with less overall harmony.

Female Venus Trine Male Mars. Here both partners find a natural compatibility as they express normal partnership roles. The male's aggressiveness complements the female's need for activity. At the same time, she cooperates and reinforces the expression of his ego. Sexual attraction is moderate while a general sense of cooperation and harmony pervades the relationship. There is pleasantness as each individual discovers the way in which he can actually be himself while sharing with another. This is an excellent aspect for an enduring friendship or relationship.

Male Venus Trine Female Jupiter. The power of love becomes the prevailing focus of the relationship. The male, through his anima, is able to receive a higher mental understanding from his mate. She generally provides the light which he receives through his sensitivities. Cooperation and expansive growth are the keynotes to this relationship through which both partners can reap great prosperity and blessings.

Female Venus Trine Male Jupiter. This aspect brings optimism, joy, and a sense of prosperity to the relationship. The free mind of the male provides the light of wisdom which warms the female's sensitivities and increases her ability to love. She admires his shining qualities and gently encourages the ideas which help him rise to his higher self. If stability is shown in other areas of his chart, this aspect can produce the happiness that makes an enduring relationship worthwhile. Thus, the symbolic gladiator carries his adoring maiden.

Male Venus Trine Female Saturn. The male learns about his own strengths through the protective and nourishing attitude of the female. She shelters and fortifies him, playing the role her father portrayed to her as a child. He may see his own father in her, thus remembering ways he was encouraged to put his creative ideas into practical form. Through patient caring and enduring love, this aspect can bring about a kind of marriage where each individual grows out of childhood patterns in order to realize fruition and personal development.

Female Venus Trine Male Saturn. The female admires the strength and protective qualities of her partner. He is her fortress, her shield, and the edifice that strengthens and firms up her character. As a father figure to his symbolic daughter, he teaches her how to direct her creativity and focus her love instincts so that they ultimately have the most meaning and purpose. Stability and enduring love can be the result of this harmonious aspect.

Male Venus Trine Female Uranus. This aspect adds interest to a relationship, but is too inconstant to plan an enduring future on. The element of fate plays a strong role in the partnership. The female's erratic qualities excite but also puzzle the male who may unconsciously identify with his anima as he tries to show his partner how she can achieve order in herself. She, at the same time, can see herself in him as he provides a nest for her flights of fancy. Sometimes this aspect causes sexual confusion, or even homosexual tendencies, as each partner questions the effectiveness of his role with the other. At best, there is an exhilarated interest, but not the firmness of understanding that can make a solid union.

Female Venus Trine Male Uranus. The female is excited by the originality, inventiveness, and unique qualities of the male. She sees him as a "tradition breaker," and in fact, her vehicle for breaking past patterns which she no longer wants. An avid interest in the arts, or the seeking of progressive comfort pervades this relationship, yet there is a note of instability here as his free mind can cause insecure feelings in his partner. There is a detached sense of aloofness through which the male preserves his unique and independent identity.

Male Venus Trine Female Neptune. This aspect helps to create a mellow flow of receptivity bringing an unconsious attunement to similar frequencies in music, the arts, and all in nature that soothes the senses. The male, through the feminine or feeling part of himself, learns about his creative possibilities. At the same time, the female sees herself through him and may find a nest for all her romanticism, sentiment, and compassion. A tone of sweetness and warmth lures the male to bathe in the soothing waters of love.

Female Venus Trine Male Neptune. The female reaches for the higher part of herself through the male. She hears the calling of his unconscious music which attracts her to him through hazy hues of colorful impressions. A romantic and dreamlike tone pervades this relationship as the female melts into the male's subtle unconsciousness. Like a changing mirror, he shows her the kaleidoscope of impressions which reflects her feelings. She is the music. He is the inspiration which fulfills the song of love whose plaintive melody is the stream of consciousness in which this relationship flows.

Male Venus Trine Female Pluto. Here the warmth of the male complements the depths in his partner. She, at the bottom of a well, sees the light he offers at the threshold of consciousness. It tempts her to transform her lower nature, to climb out of the raging inferno within her to the utter simplicity of self-acceptance. Gentle transformations bring about much growth in both partners. The male realizes the power of his ability to love and the female sees love's light at the top of the well, as they grow toward each other.

Female Venus Trine Male Pluto. From the dark roots in the soil a plant eventually blossoms. The male hunts in the dark to provide security for the woman he loves. The more he does, the more he transforms the base qualities within himself, until ultimately he becomes the Angel of Light for her to follow. In the process, she gives him warmth, enriching herself through his mysterious quest for understanding. When he sees her light at the end of the tunnel, he begins to touch the fruits of goodness that had always seemed beyond his reach as both begin to share a tremendous depth of feeling.

Venus Opposite Venus. This aspect causes the tastes and likes of each individual to be opposed to the other. In an attempt to find harmony in a relationship, it becomes difficult for both partners to be satisfied at the same time. Still, there can be a sense of objectivity here which may produce growth in both individuals. If the planets appear in masculine signs, the relationship tends to symbolize the male's weak resistance to his anima. If the planets appear in feminine signs, they show the ways in which the female is opposed to herself. Yet the mere fact that this relationship exists at all indicates how an attraction of opposite values can magnetize two individuals.

Male Venus Opposite Female Mars. The role reversals of the male and the female forces each to struggle for identity because of the anima/animus projections. Sexual attraction is strong, but the male inwardly resents the aggressive female who acts out the role he desires for himself. At the same time, she resents his submissiveness. Thus, each must make concessions to the other if this relationship is to work.

Female Venus Opposite Male Mars. This aspect increases sexual attraction but also reflects the manner in which both individuals symbolically act out the archetypal differences between the sexes. The female sees the individualistic side of the male. She needs his attention but does not know how to go after it without violating her feminine receptivity. At the same time, the male can experience feelings of rejection over what he may interpret as her indifference. This aspect brings about a tendency for misunderstanding even though both partners have good intentions.

Male Venus Opposite Female Jupiter. The love nature of the male opposes the philosophical views, attitudes, and beliefs of his mate. Although he can be overly attached to her free spirit, he may be unable to effectively pin her down to the stabilized enduring relationship he seeks. She sees the feminine side of herself in him, but it is not the kind of femininity that agrees with her philosophical outlook on life. As a result, she tends to run in many directions in order to avoid being caught in what appears to her to be a venus-fly trap. The male stands in the valley, viewing the mountain he is about to climb, that may not hold all he needs. The female, looking down at her mate, impersonally gives her wisdom, but cannot see the full value of the love or security he offers her.

Female Venus Opposite Male Jupiter. Here the female experiences the frustration of being unable to reach truth through her feelings of love. The male's free spirit and highly active mind prove to be a constant source of irritation to her. She cannot be herself without appearing to be opposed to his sense of truth and honor. As a result, she experiences the conflict between the love she feels and the light she desires. Sometimes this aspect brings about dissipation of finances, as the male spends what his mate is trying to save. The valley mother unknowingly tries to enclose the mountain whose expansive outlook fails to see her intention.

Male Venus Opposite Female Saturn. Here the male struggles with unconscious father conflicts through his anima. He feels inferior to his mate whose pretentious or overbearing nature may be too much for him. The conflict between traditional or parental strivings for practicality and a male youth's interest in the arts, aesthetics, music and expression of real feeling comes to the fore in this relationship. The female, struggling to find the artistic and natural side of herself, inwardly resents the burdens and responsibilities that she feels she must carry. As she projects these burdens on the male he, in turn, feels unappreciated for his sensitivities. Thus, the natural flow of love is impeded by a karmic learning process through which each individual must confront very difficult parts of themselves.

Female Venus Opposite Male Saturn. The female may unconsciously be aware of the manner in which her father stifled the development of her identity. As a result, she feels it necessary to prove herself to her mate. He may act out his father's role in order to keep from feeling vulnerable to the feminine aura. Karma between father and daughter roles will be acted out until each is able to appreciate and respond to the value in the other. Love is not expressed easily here for the coldness of Saturn's wall impedes the natural flow of feelings in the relationship.

Male Venus Opposite Female Uranus. This difficult aspect causes a strong and spontaneous attraction between two individuals who are basically incompatible. The more the male responds to the female's unconventionality, the more he opposes his own anima image. He can either pursue the strangeness in the female (which can, in some instances, bring out homosexual tendencies in himself) or extricate himself from her, thereby preserving his concept of "woman" for a more suitable relationship.

Female Venus Opposite Male Uranus. Here the female discovers that the sense of freedom she seeks from her mate is adverse to her own true nature. There can be strong magnetic attraction, yet at the same time, irritating conflicts in this relationship. The more she admires his spirit of originality, the more he is encouraged to rebel against her affections. The maiden feeds her Spartan so he will be strong enough in the battle but she will lose him when he discovers his strength.

Male Venus Opposite Female Neptune. In this female-oriented relationship, the male is confused by the manner in which his anima keeps eluding him. As he attempts to reflect through his mate, he tries to reach her sensitivity to the hidden feminine part of himself. Yet the more love she brings out in him, the more he loses the complete mate within himself. He is both intrigued by his mate and unconsciously annoyed with the archetypal confusion the aspect sets off. To retain a comfortable concept of "woman," he may inevitably sacrifice the woman he loves.

Female Venus Opposite Male Neptune. The female seeks to find a higher expression of her gentle compassionate nature in a male who keeps dissolving her personal efforts at winning his love. The more she chases a dream, the more she loses herself, until she ultimately becomes the dream, wishing for the person she once was. This aspect can cause self-defeating behavior in the female, while the male relates to his partner through illusions and imagery that he believes are appealing. Thus, it is difficult for both partners to achieve an enduring relationship.

Male Venus Opposite Female Pluto. This is an extremely passionate and volatile aspect which often causes breaks and separations in relationships. The male unconsciously feels the feminine side of himself and tries to destroy all he sees as weakness. She sees herself in him but may not understand the destructive force in herself that keeps fighting his giving nature. Difficult transformations can be achieved through this aspect as the powerful sexual force reaches the level of feelings, meets with opposition, and eventually manages to surface new awarenesses which produce growth.

Female Venus Opposite Male Pluto. The female feels the male passion and volatility stemming from its basest levels and forcing her through difficult changes. She gives her love while he erodes all in her that must be eliminated if she is to grow. In the process, the gentle soothing vibration of Venus feels threatened as the understanding of love is tested at its deepest levels. Reaching for her mate's approval she loses herself in the passionate throes of upheaval, which—if she can stand it—will ultimately create a new awareness. This aspect is so tumultuous that it often breaks relationships, regardless of other strengths available to the partners.

Mars Aspects

Mars Conjunct Mars. Here we have two individual egos pulling in the same direction. Competitiveness may exist but it can be directed toward a common goal. Thus, the female identifies with her animus in order to keep up with her male. By doing this, she loses some of her femininity in what can become a "brother-like" type of rivalry. Still, each pushes the other to do their best. Sexual expression can be difficult as each partner challenges the other without finding receptive surrender. This aspect can be frustrating or can stimulate great achievements for both individuals.

Male Mars Conjunct Female Jupiter. This aspect adds expansiveness to a relationship. The male finds the female inspiring, yet she must use sound judgment tempered with wisdom in order to keep the relationship from becoming excessive. There is much activity but goals have to be clearly defined. An interest in sports, games or travel is an integral part of this aspect. As both individuals activate each other, the male relates through his instincts, the female through her understanding. There is the possibility for great material wealth and spiritual growth if both individuals are wise enough to overcome any primitive or childlike impulses which may arise out of over-enthusiasm.

Female Mars Conjunct Male Jupiter. Here the female is apt to identify with her animus figure, and as she does, tends to push her mate to his higher mind. She can force him to realize the Athenean God-like qualities she desires. Although she can be overly aggressive, the male understands her instincts. This heightens the activity of the relationship and produces a great deal of sparks and movement. Much learning occurs as the female absorbs her mate's philosophical attitude, while he, in turn, sees the way she activates his ideas. This aspect may be difficult sexually because of excessive uncontrolled enthusiasm! Each individual can easily go through the other without truly meeting.* If a sense of balance is maintained, there can be excitement amidst a growing relationship.

Male Mars Conjunct Female Saturn. The female adds realism and purpose to the often child-like impulses of her mate. He sees her as the controlling factor in the relationship but he respects her wisdom and sense of propriety. His youthful desires stimulate her while she provides a secure base for his ego. This is a particularly karmic aspect in which the female takes on the father role. She leads her mate to the wisdom and dignity she believes he deserves. He tries to earn her respect as if she were his father, yet he can only do this by striving to achieve her principles. This aspect is usually found in relationships where the female is trying to correct an ego problem from her childhood. She focuses the male, directing his energies into fruitful areas in the same way she was taught to point her own ego. The relationship will take on the nuances of the female's ancestral background. Thus, against the backdrop of her traditions, both will strive to build a future.

Female Mars Conjunct Male Saturn. This is an important karmic aspect. Here the male must be a father to himself as he reenacts the blending of impulse with the wisdom he was taught in his childhood. He sees the female as a reflection of his own ego and tries to direct her in the ways which he has found meaningful. She in turn stimulates him through her youthful vitality and exuberance. However, she may not experience either her femininity or even her true identity, since

*See *The Astrology of Sexuality,* by Martin Schulman, Samuel Weiser, Inc., York Beach, Maine, 1982.

it is the male's background and karmic task which create the setting for this relationship. She may impulsively try to push him to overcome heavy or decadent ways. She may even take on some of his karmic burdens. Yet ultimately, it is his delays and sense of purpose which add thoughtfulness and meaning to this learning relationship.

Male Mars Conjunct Female Uranus. This aspect adds an exciting and electrifying stimulus to a relationship. It signifies "courtship" as the male is attracted to the challenge of winning the attentions of the erratic female. She tries to be detached but the more she is, the more she inadvertently attracts the male. Both individuals energize each other. The ultimate result after the sparks of excitement have waned is that the male (after experiencing much turmoil) realizes that in seeking a lover he has found a friend.

Female Mars Conjunct Male Uranus. The female aggressively seeks to win the rather detached attentions of the male. She is out of her role and may take on his identity in order to create the tangible reality she needs. Thus, the relationship can be exciting, but the female must learn how to expect the unexpected. She tries to make the male more personal and more intimately involved in an effort to create a closer relationship. Although he enjoys her aggressiveness, he can only take it in small doses and he may desire intermittent breaks from the partnership in order to preserve his sense of freedom.

Male Mars Conjunct Female Neptune. This is a balancing aspect as the male tries to find the object of his aggressiveness in the female while she in turn attempts to soothe his fiery nature. In effect, he powers her dreams and strives to activate her imagination. She may feel that he is moving too fast for her but she is powerless to change this quality in the relationship. Mars is the planet of desire. Neptune symbolizes the dissolving of the desire nature. Through these two opposites each partner centers the other into more realistic expectations from life.

Female Mars Conjunct Male Neptune. The female may be unconsciously identifying with her animus and acts out the male role. She activates the dreams of her mate and leads him to activate his own dormant instincts. If he doesn't resent her, this can be a constructive aspect in which inspiration and action cojoin to form an inspirationally activated partnership.

Male Mars Conjunct Female Pluto. This aspect adds intensity and passion to a relationship. There may be decisive finality to things which enables both individuals to progress into the future. The female keeps breaking from the past while the male assertively seeks the future. In this way both partners act as a regenerative force to each other. Sexuality can be intense and because of it, the karmic patterns of the past can surface, be eliminated, and replaced with a new exciting freshness of future expectation.

Female Mars Conjunct Male Pluto. This is an intensely passionate aspect in which the female abandons her traditional role and identifies instead with her animus. From her strength, the male finds new ways in which he can activate his unconscious depths. Thus, she becomes his motivation. He is the diamond in the rough and it is through her incessant probing that he is able to provide the power which ultimately regenerates both. As his dormant potential is brought to life through her demands, there tends to be a great deal of turmoil, but the end result can be an enormous amount of dynamic growth.

Mars Square Mars. Both partners experience tension as different ego needs clash with each other. The female has to be overly assertive to compete with the challenges her mate presents. Both individuals fight for identity in what may prove to be a stimulating but also combative relationship. Tempers run high and a general sense of snappiness or irritability can be the result of neither individual sensing their own validity. At best, this is a difficult aspect for an enduring relationship.

Male Mars Square Female Jupiter. This aspect can bring about a great deal of activity without actual purpose. The instincts and impulses of the male contradict the ideas or philosophy of the female. He tries to assert himself without clearly seeing her point of view. Thus, the male pursues the female whose outlook seems to be just beyond his reach. There can be strong differences in beliefs which make this relationship difficult to endure, particularly since the female tends to judge the motivations of her mate. Impatience and frustration tend to push each person towards personal individuality rather than creating a smooth, enduring partnership.

Female Mars Square Male Jupiter. The female aggressively pursues her mate while he seeks his freedom. This aspect can indicate an antagonizing relationship because each partner lacks patience with the other. Individuality runs high and there is a general lack of receptiveness which makes an enduring relationship difficult.

Male Mars Square Female Saturn. In this karmic aspect both the male and female are drawn to each other through mutual lessons which they both have to learn. There are abrasive struggles as the male tries to impress his mate and finds that her standards are in conflict with his efforts. She may try to control, center, and focus his ego which she thinks may be too immature. Unconsciously acting as a father figure, she becomes the guiding force for the relationship. Her demands, however, are felt as being unusually heavy for he questions her source of wisdom, her sense of propriety, as well as the very direction in life she appears to be moving in. This is an achievement aspect. If each partner can understand the other's function as being meaningful even though different, then the relationship can be built from a solid foundation. The female inherited a sense of wisdom from her father and needs to use it to establish a frame of reference for grounding the male's impulsiveness. She must be the backbone that he both resents and needs if he is to find the purpose in life that he seeks.

Female Mars Square Male Saturn. In this karmic aspect, the male sees his own youth repeated through the female's impetuous nature. Acting in the tradition of his father, he strives to control her ego. At the same time, she unconsciously identifies with his youth. His real struggle, and the unconscious reason he enters this relationship in the first place, is to learn how to put effective controls on himself. Once he does this, great meaning and purpose can come out of this partnership.

Male Mars Square Female Uranus. This aspect creates an extremely hectic and volatile relationship. While there is a great deal of excitement, sensation, and intense attraction, an erratic quality is present which creates unexpected and unpredictable turns of events. The male may be disappointed because of his mate's changeable sexual nature. She has the power to attract but not the ability to surrender. Although many sparks fly with this aspect, there may not be enough stability for an enduring partnership.

Female Mars Square Male Uranus. With this aspect, the female tends to unconsciously take on a male role, sacrificing her femininity in an effort to reach her mate. Yet his aloof sense of detachment and philosophically impersonal attitudes irk her, causing her to feel that her efforts are wasted. The male retains his independence while the female is faced with the challenge of retaining some grip on herself while she tries to conquer his haphazard freedom-loving instinct. As a result, this relationship can be particularly one-sided; not only lacking a firm base, but also missing the fair give-and-take qualities that are the very essence of an enduring partnership.

Male Mars Square Female Neptune. This aspect is extremely difficult. The direction in which the relationship is moving becomes confused as the female's fantasies tend to blur her partner's drive. He seeks to lead but she cannot understand his purpose. There is a lack of communication as well as purpose here that causes feelings of isolation in both partners.

Female Mars Square Male Neptune. In this relationship, both partners experience role reversal. The female takes on the male ego as she tries to compensate for the strength she feels he lacks. As a result, he can easily come to resent the way in which she interrupts his wispy fantasies. The more she desires progress, the more he attempts to escape into his own secluded private reality. She may lose her way with him as well as the sense of direction in which both could be moving. Although there is both sexual and sensual energy in this aspect, it lacks the substance from which a lasting relationship is formed.

Male Mars Square Female Pluto. This is one of the most difficult aspects in a relationship. The survival nature in each individual clashes with the other as both attempt to stay in touch with a personal sense of self. He overtly strives to assert his independence while she does the same thing subconsciously. There may be a great deal of powerful intensity as well as many altercations as each tries to conquer the other. Passionate sexuality can ultimately transform the female into enlightenment, for she is forever destroying the past while the male is paving the way for the future. Unless there are other constructive and strong conjunctions between the two charts, there might be no common meeting ground for either her past or his future. As a result, this aspect takes on the harsh reality of brutal self-transformations which can create too much turbulence for an enduring relationship.

Female Mars Square Male Pluto. This is an extremely volatile aspect as the female acts through an identification with her animus and loses herself in the unconscious motives of her mate. Both partners struggle for power, each hoping to conquer the other. The male can be perverse if he feels his hidden needs thwarted. Thus, intense sexuality may become the battleground used to fight out the basic incompatibility of this aspect. Ultimately the male will be transformed as he realizes his new depths. But seldom does he grow closer in consciousness to the female, no matter how much he changes or grows.

Mars Trine Mars. With this aspect, both individuals are able to retain their unique independence while cooperating with each other. The relationship is male-oriented insofar as a sense of progress, achievement, and the fulfillment of one's desires becomes the impetus for action. Thus, there is a great deal of movement and energizing of interests through which both individuals are able to help each other grow. The female unconsciously identifies with her animus and acts out the needs of the male. If she has brothers, the relationship may become her vehicle for meeting challenges she was unable to conquer in the past, thus finding a new sense of worth in herself. Through a series of beginnings, this partnership can retain a youthful freshness which stimulates both individuals.

Male Mars Trine Female Jupiter. This aspect creates an interest in sports, travel and leisure. There is an intense quality to the relationship, but it is pointed in light and easy directions. The female is able to teach her mate how to reach beyond his grasp. She helps him unfold his consciousness and shows him how the mind understands what the ego acts out. He in turn stimulates her thought processes which provide more ideas that create progress in the relationship. There is a great deal of activity and movement as both individuals help each other to expand and assert their sense of individuality.

Female Mars Trine Male Jupiter. The female may identify with her animus to provide ego strength and a sense of one-mindedness to her mate. He sees many possibilities but needs her as a point of focus. In turn, she receives an optimistic outlook for her expectations from him. If realistic goals are set, there can be opportunity here for achievement. If goals are absent, however, a sense of impatience and irritability can destroy what might otherwise be a fruitful partnership.

Male Mars Trine Female Saturn. Here the male looks to his mate for guidance. She is his anchor, his source, his sense of continuity. As he learns how to blend his impulses with her realistic sense of wisdom, both can reach great achievements together. He strives for the future while she solidifies the past. There can be a weak karmic link here insofar as both individuals are learning how to focus and dedicate energy toward something worthwhile. On an unconscious level, the male is cooperating with his symbolic father. The female may sacrifice her feminine self for that which appears to have greater meaning. This is an excellent aspect for two individuals who choose to work together.

Female Mars Trine Male Saturn. In this aspect, the female responds to the symbolic father-like demands of her mate. He in turn sees the ways in which youth and age can create a spectrum of understanding through which a broad scope of wisdom may be developed. The female is anxious to move forward. The male sees his own impulsive nature in her. At the same time he must guide her in traditional ways which will assure success to her activities. In essence, he helps to direct the expression of her ego. In a karmic sense the female cooperates with her father image and although her mate may not recognize her feminine role, he nevertheless sees the potential in her ego. In past lives she developed the need to identify with a principle, an idea or a tradition that extended beyond her personal self. Through this relationship she reaches beyond her years, striving to achieve the stature, honor, and meaning that only progressing through the wisdom of advanced age can bring her.

Male Mars Trine Female Uranus. This aspect produces a hectic and turbulent relationship. The male acts through his ego to achieve an impersonal understanding of his mate. She provides the objectivity which balances his subjective outlook. Through complementing each other's sense of progress, the relationship takes on the quality of two youthful children eagerly trying to taste their future.

Female Mars Trine Male Uranus. This aspect can help the female achieve independence through contact with her mate's liberal attitudes. He can use objectivity to explain her actions and motivations. She may enter this relationship much too close to her desire nature, and becomes overinvolved, convoluted or enmeshed in things to the point where she cannot see herself. The male can help her disentangle herself so she can see more universal concepts. Both partners can learn the advantages of developing a less personal ego in this relationship.

Male Mars Trine Female Neptune. Here the ego drive of the male is complemented by the inspirational dreams of the female. She adds color and texture to all he does as she helps to enhance his impression of himself. He in turn is able to show her how to activate her dreams so that a purposeful reality can be created. Although he is brusque and to the point while she is vague and elusive, there is an intriguing sense of sexual magnetism here, for she is like the butterfly that stays close enough to be almost caught.

Female Mars Trine Male Neptune. The female unconsciously identifies with her animus. Taking the lead in the relationship, she tries to activate the docile male. He absorbs her drive, calming her while adding insight and vision to her instincts. Still, she seeks progress while he enjoys fantasy. If his fantasies are creative, however, she has the power to activate them.

Male Mars Trine Female Pluto. This aspect increases the sexual tone of the relationship. The male sees the depths in his mate and because of his intensity, is able to surface the hidden qualities in her unconscious. She goes through many changes, stripping away her past while he gives her the incentive to move towards the future. As a result, there can be a great deal of dynamic growth in this relationship.

Female Mars Trine Male Pluto. Here the female identifies with her animus and leads the male through great transformations. He strips away the shackles of a useless past while she pushes him to a more self-centered future. Sexual interest runs high as both partners are participating in the regenerative process. Through her strength and his depth this can be an extremely dynamic relationship. It can propel the male far from his roots and closer to the desires of his mate. In effect, she complements his needs which surface through her momentum.

Mars Opposite Mars. This is an extremely difficult aspect. Both egos experience a tug or war in trying to realize personal desires. The female is out of her role and must overly assert herself if she is to be heard. For every action there is an equal and opposite reaction. As a result, the more she asserts herself, the more the male asserts himself in the opposite direction. There can be a powerful sexual attraction here but it is often too intense for the individuals to understand. The female sees herself as so wrapped up in her mate's ego that she may eventually feel that it takes too much of a sacrifice on her part to make this relationship work.

Male Mars Opposite Female Jupiter. This aspect causes a scattering of energies along with difficulty in finding the actual point of the relationship. The male is functioning through his ego, the female through her higher mind. But neither her ideas nor his impulses seem to be on the same wavelength. As a result, his efforts to impress her may lead him off his course making it difficult for both to understand their sense of purpose.

Female Mars Opposite Male Jupiter. Here the female tends to over identify with her animus. She tries to impress the male but his wisdom and knowledge may be beyond her comprehension. She views things subjectively while he has the ability to detach because he can see things on a higher level. Both fight for personal freedom but it is the female who is more apt to be hurt for she is more deeply involved in the relationship than her uncommitted mate.

Male Mars Opposite Female Saturn. The male struggles to extricate himself from the father figure he sees in his mate. She represents a collection of crystallized rules, traditions and formalities which he would rather not be a part of. She views him as being overly youthful and irresponsible. Because these two points of view are so different, much irritation can result. The male is confronted with a choice between self-expression or proving himself as an authority figure. In a karmic sense, he has invited this relationship so he can ultimately learn how to break the shackles of his inhibitions and be his own person. Thus, the more the female tries to enclose, limit, and keep him within the confines of her expectations, the more she learns that it is impossible to ever control another person. As a result, she must ultimately set him free to gain her own sense of self-respect.

Female Mars Opposite Male Saturn. The female is out of her natural role. Because of this, she is forced to use her ego against her mate as she tries to symbolically extricate herself from his bondage. He may burden her with the weight of tradition or make her strive to find her identity. Ultimately she must learn that she is not trying to overcome a father figure but rather the limitations within herself which are holding her back. When she learns this, she will break from the excessive karmic weight of this relationship, leaving the male to understand that he, too, has learned a way to discipline himself.

Male Mars Opposite Female Uranus. This aspect creates change and unpredictability. The male tries to conquer the free spirit of the female. She is not interested, however, in being conquered. Instead, she seeks to maintain an isolated sense of individuality, avoiding intimacy and closeness. The male, too, wants to maintain his unique identity. But his desires are more intimate and personal. Thus, he sees the relationship and his role in it mostly through his ego. At the same time, the unreachable female functions through universal mind and needs a broader horizon to maintain her interest.

Female Mars Opposite Male Uranus. The female over-identifies with her animus. She battles with herself trying to understand why the male does not act as she expects. His aloofness and sense of detachment frustrate her but her need to intimately personalize challenges is constantly restimulated by his impersonal attitude. She may lose much of herself as she tries to reach the unattainable, for the male, who in the end turns out to be more of a friend than a lover, can never be the kind of man she is unconsciously trying to conquer.

Male Mars Opposite Female Neptune. This aspect often causes dishonesty. The male tries to conquer the female and more often than not, he is fooling himself. Rather than truly seeing her full being, his instinctive nature is reaching for a stereotype which may not exist. She sees his efforts but can do little to alleviate the illusion he is battling. As a result, the relationship takes on the tone of a man in armor trying to conquer a passing cloud.

Female Mars Opposite Male Neptune. Here the female is out of her natural role as she chases some impressionary illusion that her mate has given her. With all the force she can muster, she tries to rend the veil of this illusion. The more she tries, however, the more she loses herself in what can ultimately be a disappointing experience.

Male Mars Opposite Female Pluto. This aspect causes volatile tensions within a relationship. There can be cruelty, hate, and possibly even violence as the male insistently prods and pushes the female to realize all that must be changed if she is to experience a rebirth in consciousness. She may resent the crudeness of his onslaughts and ultimately come to feel that all the relationship has to offer is punishment. Sexuality can be extremely intense but there is a crudeness to it because neither individual is really treating self or partner with kindness and decency.

Female Mars Opposite Male Pluto. Here the female over-emphasizes the masculine role. Everything becomes exaggerated as she tries to reach her mate at the very core of his unconscious being. Thus she goads and provokes him, as if unconsciously blaming him for her lack of femininity. The male feels himself transforming, but cannot relate to the tantrums and temper displays that he sees in his mate. There is an animalistic quality in this aspect which tends to bring out the very worst in both partners. If other aspects in the chart show good sense and reason, then much can be learned here in a very short period of time.

ASPECTS
TO THE OUTER PLANETS

Jupiter Aspects

Jupiter Conjunct Jupiter. This aspect adds optimism, bright-ness, and good fortune to a relationship. Although there can be excess, it is often balanced by the ability of both partners to keep things on a light level. Having the same basic philosophy on life, there is much promise for an interesting, expansive and growing relationship. Usually this aspect indicates the partners are close in age and share the same generational outlook.

Male Jupiter Conjunct Female Saturn. This is a balancing aspect in which the excessive optimism of the male is kept in check by the sober and responsible way of the female. He may seek external experiences in order to brighten his outlook. She provides the inner core which stabilizes him and gives him strength. If the male can learn to overcome boredom, and if the female learns not to be irritated by his constant changes of direction, this aspect can produce a relationship with much inherent wisdom. Honor and truth can join with dignity and purpose. The female, through unconscious identification with the father, will seek to preserve the sterling qualities she admires in her mate. There is karma here and she must go through much effort in order to keep the male from scattering himself or wasting his energies while she slowly shows him the essential purpose and meaning of his life.

Female Jupiter Conjunct Male Saturn. The male balances the female as he shows her the importance of patience, discrimination and responsibility. He strives to teach her the values which will give her substantial meaning. If she has the patience to listen to his teachings, this relationship can slowly mold itself on the principles of truth, wisdom and the kind of substantial meaning that endures. There is the possibility of achieving something which can bring about much fame and honor.

Male Jupiter Conjunct Female Uranus. This is a mind aspect. It raises the consciousness of a relationship while bringing new understandings through the enlightened intellects of both partners. Telepathic understandings are instantaneous as a result of the excellent communication that this aspect can produce. The expansive nature of the male meets with the freeing and innovative intellect of his mate. There can be much inventiveness adding to mental stimulation, yet sexuality can be difficult as the freeing quality of the aspect tends to loosen interest in physical appetites.

Female Jupiter Conjunct Male Uranus. Here the higher mind of the female expands the intellect of the male helping both to experience a changing and growing consciousness. This is a non-possessive relationship in which both individuals experience freedom of mind. There is a great deal of movement, activity and interest but a tendency to scatter energies has to be watched. Fits and starts of exuberance can both heighten awareness and create frustrations. The non-sexual nature of this aspect makes it excellent for a platonic friendship in which each individual learns and grows from the other.

Male Jupiter Conjunct Female Neptune. The higher mind of the male blends with the intuitive capacity of the female to create a sense of telepathic understanding. The female is dependent upon the male for her truths while his optimism is enhanced by the strength of her belief in him. There is a great deal of astral projection here, as both individuals tend to experience a discontent with the present and may try to reach for the imagined visions of things beyond their immediate horizon.

Female Jupiter Conjunct Male Neptune. The female brightens the spirit of her mate. She carries the truth of his impressions and teaches him how to release the excess of all he absorbs through his sensitivities. He in turn provides the intuition which adds depth and insight to her perceptions.

Male Jupiter Conjunct Female Pluto. Here the light optimistic attitudes of the male blend with the depth and insight of the female to produce a powerfully intense relationship. He has scope and perspective; she sees the undercurrents in life. While she teaches him the finality of his truths, he is able to expand the insights which she would otherwise only glimpse. This is a powerfully regenerative aspect which brings out a desire to experience a progressive future in both individuals.

Female Jupiter Conjunct Male Pluto. The female helps to expand the consciousness of her mate through her higher mind. Through the depths of his understanding and the broadness of her perceptions, there can be a profound sense of wisdom in this relationship. She opens his consciousness providing the light he needs to transform his soul.

Jupiter Square Jupiter. This aspect causes tension and frustration. The individualistic attitudes and opinions of both partners strive for recognition. As a result, the tendency for a clashing of personalities makes this relationship extremely difficult. The greatest problem occurs because both individuals have different philosophical outlooks on life; this difference becomes ultimately more important than any attraction which might exist between them.

Male Jupiter Square Female Saturn. The philosophy of the male clashes with the traditional background or ancestral lineage of the female. He seeks an open consciousness based on learning, growing, and expanding, while she holds on to the past and may close herself off from bright opportunities. She may try to preserve what is already solidified while he wants to use his higher mind to grow beyond his current security.

In a karmic sense, the female is continuing a linear thread from her ancestry. The thoughts of her mate often represent an attitude which contradicts her sense of form, custom or structure. There can be ethnic or cultural differences here and these differences must be understood on an impersonal level if this relationship is to work.

Female Jupiter Square Male Saturn. The female seeks freedom, lightness and ease while the male is firmly rooted in his past. Taking on the father role, he tends to "freeze" time at some historical point in the past which was significant for him on some karmic level. He tries to continue past traditions, customs or attitudes which were socially acceptable. The more he does this, however, the more the female asserts her need for freedom. She seeks the openness of learning, growing, and wondering what is beyond each new horizon. He tries to structure the future into the karmic past.

There is a bondage involving ideas in this relationship and if both individuals are to experience growth it will be brought to light through the female. There is a teaching karma here and her learning must unfold from the historical time setting that the male creates. He may favor a particular culture, civilization, or set rules and traditions that come from his ancestry. She must loosen and dissipate these crystallized rules in order to balance the relationship in a realistic current setting.

Male Jupiter Square Female Uranus. This is a frivolous and hectic aspect adding a great deal of movement and activity to a relationship. There are impersonal differences which may not be easy to overcome. Both partners have a strong sense of individuality, independence, and freedom of mind. Each, however, tends to invade the psychic space of the other. As a result, there may be a stimulation of nervous anxiety along with an avoidance of feelings. This energy makes it difficult for each individual to understand or empathize with the other.

The relationship can be exciting but seldom enduring, for each partner may discover he is more attached to an idea or a way of life than to his mate.

Female Jupiter Square Male Uranus. Here the female's attitude and outlook contradict the male's underlying belief in himself. She can be overly righteous while he seeks the freedom that he is accustomed to, while tending to object to her judgmental manner. He may impersonally detach himself from the relationship, scattering her sense of purpose along with her thought projections for the future. Both partners can learn a great deal from each other but the amount of mental frustration that this aspect creates makes it difficult for either individual to feel secure.

Male Jupiter Square Female Neptune. This aspect causes spiritual discontent. The male seeks his truths in the mystical impressions he receives from the female. She has difficulty believing his sincerity, however, as he appears to be too frivolous to understand her depth. At the same time his definitive sense of right and wrong may often be confused by her nebulous outlook. She tries to show him the spirit or essence of his rule systems—she wants him to understand that the essence is more important than the literal ways he understands life. The male can grow in this relationship, if he keeps an open mind and frees himself from possessive or prejudicial attitudes.

Female Jupiter Square Male Neptune. The female tries to find inspiration through her mate. She may seek either a psychic or intuitive confirmation of what she believes to be her truths. But the male may only perceive the "surfacy" manner in which she looks at things and may find it difficult to accept her sincerity. He believes that she needs to develop more depth while she loses patience because of his lack of spontaneity. This aspect is a difficult one, causing strain in the attitude and belief systems of both partners.

Male Jupiter Square Female Pluto. The male may put in a lot of mental energy trying to enlighten the female. At the same time, she strives to add depth to what she feels he perceives only superficially as truth. Both partners are looking at life from different vantage points. The male sees expediency and the lighter side of things. The female sees the depths and the real transformations that one must make in order to achieve spiritual growth. Because of these two different levels of consciousness, the relationship may develop an undercurrent which often causes disagreements, discontent, friction, malevolence, and eventual separation.

Female Jupiter Square Male Pluto. The female tries to enlighten her mate. She may see him struggling through the depths, but she doesn't understand the reasons why he digs so deeply for the answers which are so readily apparent to her. At the same time, he feels that her hastiness in forming opinions or attitudes indicates that she misses the true essence of life at its very core. She may live in an open expansive consciousness while he peers into the closed and hidden corners to find his truths. The greatest difficulty occurs when both partners believe that there is a finality to their own opinions. As a result, minor disagreements become difficult to smooth over.

Jupiter Trine Jupiter. This aspect enhances luck; it brings opportunity, expansiveness and popular feelings into the relationship. Both the male and female are able to complement each other through their higher minds. As a result, there is an ease which allows each individual to retain freedom of mind while feeling in harmony with the beliefs of the other.

Male Jupiter Trine Female Saturn. The expansive nature of the male is complemented by the conservative wisdom of his mate. She presents a firm base from which he can build. As a result his hopes and wishes are kept in practical proportions because of her realistic attitude. She may play the role of father, thereby forming the center of consciousness for the relationship. Her protective yin attitudes act as a perfect balance for the male's yang quality which is forever seeking outward expression. There is a positive karma here as the ancestral lineage of the female blends with the cultural attitudes of her mate. She provides the foundation upon which his ideas can expand. As a result, this aspect adds dignity, mutual respect and honor to what could be a very fulfilling partnership.

Female Jupiter Trine Male Saturn. The female is able to show the male his own value because of her openness and sincerity. He may act out the role of his father, or "father-like" figures, in order to impress his mate with a sense of honor and dignity that is slightly beyond his grasp. Yet the more the female expands his consciousness, the more he grows to see the important reasons for rules, traditions or customs that are ingrained within his being.

A karma exists here and it combines judgment and wisdom. The female plays a constructive role while her mate plays a more receptive one—symbolizing the changing of established structure—yet each balances the other as they achieve vision, foresight and perspective. This is an excellent aspect for a balanced and growing partnership.

Male Jupiter Trine Female Uranus. The free spirit of the male stimulates the intellect of his partner. She provides ideas which activate him, while he helps her to expand her consciousness. Both partners are highly individualistic but their philosophies and ideas are harmonious. Thus, while each respects the psychic space of the other, there is growth potential along with optimistic expectations for the future. Both partners see restlessness in the other but this can usually manifest in activities (sports, travel and entertainment), which add excitement to the relationship. This aspect can work well in a two-career marriage.

Female Jupiter Trine Male Uranus. The female broadens her mate's intellect. Her openness and free spirit inspire his sense of originality and ingenuity. Thus, she tends to bring out higher qualities in him which might otherwise not manifest. He, in turn, understands her need for space and can relate to her fairly, without being possessive or one-sided. There can be excitement without commitment, for both partners are committed to the impersonal idea of individual free expression.

Male Jupiter Trine Female Neptune. This aspect expands dreams, hopes and wishes. Through his optimism and eagerness the male inspires the female's beliefs. She colors his ideas, giving them more depth and feeling. Spiritual principles and basic philosophies are in agreement which makes this partnership easy. The main difficulty to watch for, however, is that effortlessness can lead to laziness. It is important to keep goals and ultimate objectives in mind. Expanded feelings can lead both partners to create a distinct reality as a couple and this reality seems better than the realities of others. Whether this is based on an illusion or the actual facts, it is important for both individuals to keep their feet on the ground.

Female Jupiter Trine Male Neptune. This aspect creates an expansive relationship. There can be a flowing sense of spirituality as the female searches for truth while her understandings can be verified by her mate's intuition. He sees the essence of things and she sees the opportunities. Both partners give freely to each other in what seems to be a higher and more expansive sense of reality than what each could experience alone. The male lives in a cloud while his mate provides the silver lining. If both individuals are practical, this can be an excellent aspect for a growing and learning relationship.

Male Jupiter Trine Female Pluto. The male is supported by the female. She provides the depth upon which his understandings develop. He encourages her seeking. Both are in search of all that is just beyond immediate understanding. The female sees reality in vertical layers while the male retains a horizontal perspective. Thus, he can see the breadth and scope of implications that arise from her depths. When these two viewpoints of reality (vertical and horizontal) are in harmony with each other, the true mystical meaning of the "Cross" is revealed.

Pluto symbolizes the death of the Christ, while Jupiter represents the resurrection. In this symbolic re-enactment, the female, by destroying parts of her past, is able to create room in her mate's consciousness for his spirit to experience rebirth.

Female Jupiter Trine Male Pluto. The male provides a proving ground that the female can use as she learns to expand her consciousness. He strips away the sham and veils of illusion, enabling her to see the light. In doing this, he may put her through many tests—for she must learn how to add depth to her breadth of vision. Both material and spiritual wealth may occur each time obstacles are overcome. This is a special aspect. It puts stumbling blocks in the way of a smoothly-running relationship, yet it also gives both partners the strength and ability to transcend these obstacles—almost welcoming them as challenges that can be changed into stepping stones towards illumination.

Jupiter Opposite Jupiter. Two different philosophies clash. Energies can be scattered and purpose can be dissipated. Both partners need freedom and tend to hold on to autonomous principles, creating a veritable tug of war on the mental plane. The result is usually frustration and anxiety as each individual would like confirmation of their attitudes from the other. Much growth can be achieved, however, through controversy, opposition, and debate. If the relationship is to work, each partner must be able to see value in the attitudes and opinions of the other.

Male Jupiter Opposite Female Saturn. This is a karmic aspect. The female, while playing the father role, tests the male's sincerity. Like Zeus, above the laws of fate, the male protests against his mate while she tries to test his position. As both partners question each other's authority, they inadvertently bring each other to higher levels of consciousness. The relationship may be extremely difficult, but it can be rewarding as each individual discovers his own true station in life.

Ideas and principles battle with each other. The female may attempt to personalize her life because of her family lineage, ancestry in this life, or the doctrines, customs and traditions which she experienced in another life that may have contradicted the culture she lived in then. Through her mate she keeps questioning and testing the validity of societies, laws and the ways of civilization. She has her rules, and because they worked in the past, she intends to make them work for her now. The male has different ideas about what one's path in life should be. As a result, this aspect tends to cause conflict, usually of a religious or cultural nature, that demands understanding from both partners if the relationship is to evolve.

Female Jupiter Opposite Male Saturn. The male takes on the father role. In a past incarnation he may have been in a position which enabled him to form opinions, beliefs, and a lifestyle which was adverse to his culture. He continues this outlook in this relationship, seeing the female as a threat to all he has already formed. She may try to escape the bondage of any rules which limit her sense of freedom. She finds principles and ideas which negate all that the male stands for, in order to loosen and dissipate his tight, enclosed consciousness. The more he tests the value of current culture through her, the more she shows him the folly of trying to impose stoic ways. She finds loopholes in his arguments, flaws in his reasoning, and does everything she can to dissipate his strength. She is leaving a bondage karma behind, but must experience this kind of relationship to gain the strength that will ultimately bring her freedom.

Male Jupiter Opposite Female Uranus. This is an extremely difficult aspect. Both partners have different beliefs and mental outlooks. Anxiety, nervousness, and a general state of restlessness pervade the daily course of events as the relationship takes on the nuance of two individual rollercoasters moving in opposite directions. The male sees the value in the quantity of his experiences. The female seeks originality. As a result, the relationship will be highly active, but often so erratic and unpredictable that it doesn't provide lasting security for either partner.

Female Jupiter Opposite Male Uranus. The restless nature of the female combines with the erratic qualities of the male and produces an unpredictable relationship. There is much attraction and mental stimulation, but rather than a free flowing exchange of ideas, there is a tendency for a basic lack of communication. Both individuals talk *at* each other instead of *to* each other. The female can be absorbed in her philosophies and opinions, while the male (who bores easily) tends to detach himself from her ideas. Impatience, intolerance, and the distance created because of an impersonal detachment must be overcome if this relationship is to work.

Male Jupiter Opposite Female Neptune. This aspect causes spiritual conflict. The male sees himself as representing truth and light, but at the same time he cannot help but feel that the female symbolizes illusion, deceit, and the inability to know truth. In reality, however, her understanding is on a higher level. She attunes herself to the essence of truth and can transcend the male's attitudes of "right" and "wrong." The more she tries to free herself from his influence and outlook, the more she realizes the difference between society's law and God's law. In the process two different levels of consciousness emerge. The male can see overt truth, but his mate understands truth even in darkness. Thus, she can be a threat to his sense of honor, while also being a magnet for his desire to understand the deeper mysteries of life.

Female Jupiter Opposite Male Neptune. The female sees the male as someone who dissolves her sense of truth. His evasive and elusive ways confuse and mystify her. She may believe that she must teach him the value of honesty. At the same time, his higher self may be teaching her a more intuitive sense of honesty, based on the lessons of compassion or how to blend with another rather than righteously judging them. He may test her sincerity, her love and her divine spirit, offering himself as a sacrifice for what in fact may be her greatest spiritual challenge.

Male Jupiter Opposite Female Pluto. In this relationship, the forces of light and darkness oppose each other. The male is fighting for his honor and tries to keep himself from stooping to nefarious methods of meeting his mate's challenges. She competes with him, often using hidden tactics, for she feels inferior to his light. The goal of both may be to "win," but each partner ultimately winds up with himself, rather than whatever his original goal was. As a result it becomes more important *how* the battles are fought, rather than who actually won. This aspect is often found in a testing relationship, where growth, changes, and transformations occur through strife over the basic principles of the partners.

Female Jupiter Opposite Male Pluto. The female tries to assert her principles amidst the eroding undercurrent of the male who is constantly trying to transform all she thinks. He may attempt to destroy her for any principles she espouses but does not live by. Thus, she tries to counterbalance the destructiveness she sees in him. She grows spiritually by finding truths that he cannot tear down. In the process, strife and hardship cause individual struggles as each tries to find a personal meaning to life.

Saturn Aspects

Aspects to Saturn indicate crystallized karmic conditions which must be surfaced and then worked through. These conditions are particularly strong in Saturn conjunctions, which tend to bind individuals together until the karma is dissolved. As a result, this kind of conjunction can be the reason why some relationships have an enduring quality even though they are not neccessarily easy.

Relationships, partnerships, and marriages that are formed through a Saturn tie always have a special meaning.

There is usually some uncultivated quality present which will mature through time. The following aspects should be studied carefully. In those instances where they apply, these aspects will not only reveal the deep meaning that can unfold in a relationship, but they also contain the very essence of individual karmic evolution. A person may be seeking a certain meaning or understanding for years (or lifetimes), but may only come to really see it because of a relationship with a person whose chart activates their Saturn.

Saturn Conjunct Saturn. This aspect can occur in any relationship when both partners are the same age.* As a result, there is a tendency for each to identify through the other with both the historical content of their lives and the meaning of past experiences. Each adds form, structure, and purpose to the other as they mutually validate and confirm common reasons for their existence. A bond of cultural and civilized values is shared by both. Through similar hero or mentor identifications, both individuals stand for similar or complementary principles and meaning in life. This aspect also indicates similar roots in a past incarnation. The female rises above the importance of her femininity to find the real meaning of her relationship with her father. This extends beyond her current-life father, however, for it is her remembrance of status and security from the past that she is seeking to strengthen now. Both partners may have carried important responsibilities in another life, for there is an affinity toward protecting that which has already been established. In some instances, this aspect appears in relationships where both partners feel they must carry on a tradition to which they are karmically committed. It may be a "family-name" or an idea, or a part of the culture for which they both feel responsible, perhaps as a result of a past incarnation promise to someone who had authority over them. In this relationship, each will add strength and power to the other in preserving the tradition which is so important to them.

*It also occurs in those relationships where one partner is approximately twenty-eight years older than the other. In this instance, there is a cyclical repetition of karma. Both individuals have similar experiences, but at different times in their lives.

Male Saturn Conjunct Female Uranus. The male adds wisdom, form and purpose to the ideas of his mate. At the same time, she has come into his life to change his sense of meaning and direction. All that he has called his roots will be redirected to an area which he may have never even considered, but which will become ultimately more important to him than whatever he is basing his current sense of meaning on. As she frees his ties to the past, the relationship takes on the nuance of a crossroads in life; a turning point where the male, guided by her understanding of the future, will shake loose from all that formerly gave him security in order to find a new karmic path. This aspect symbolizes the end of one karmic pattern and the beginning of another. The relationship will involve a series of difficult changes for the male as his new direction in life unfolds. He may have to learn how to depersonalize authority figures or ideas which have been holding him back, and as he does this, learn how to overcome fears and insecurities. And he must develop an entirely new outlook on life if he is to experience the new cycle he is preparing for.

Female Saturn Conjunct Male Uranus. In this aspect, the female is experiencing a change in her karmic pattern. Whatever she thought or believed for years is at a crossroads. Her ideas regarding respectability, pleasing, or living for authority figures, or upholding traditions will be shaken to the very core by her mate. Ultimately, she can free herself from a finished karma of the past and begin a new path. The male who frees her will become more conventional as a result of this relationship. Because of a powerful clashing of ideologies, both partners experience a lifestyle to which they are unaccustomed. This aspect is often difficult, but because of the obstacles it creates, great changes can occur. The female's change will be permanent. The male will have learned the importance of substance, form, and the power of limitation.

Usually this is not a permanent relationship, but rather a karmic interchange occurring at a specific time in life when lessons are ready to be learned. Although it is the female who experiences a new direction in life, the male will feel the effect of the relationship for a longer period of time afterward.

Male Saturn Conjunct Female Neptune. This is the most mystifying aspect that can occur in a relationship. Strange or even miraculous events become everyday occurrences. Whatever the female has always dreamed or fantasized about for years prior to this relationship can manifest as a result of the interaction between them. He crystallizes her imagination. She may dream of flowers in the afternoon, and he materializes them the same evening. It is even more amazing that the flowers he brings her will be exactly as she imagined them. The ESP levels of both individuals are karmically linked to each other here, so that fulfillment of what is imagined can be possible.

While the female keeps her head in the clouds, the male is firmly rooted in reality. Spirit and form combine in this "dreams come true" aspect. Usually a relationship of this kind occurs in the life of a female who has an extremely vivid imagination (with great creative potential), but who has been unable to focus her dreams or even see their connection with the real world. Through this relationship, she learns that her dreams have very material effects or consequences. The male helps her focus her imagination, bringing to fruition that which is of value, while teaching her how to discard that which is not. He tests her beliefs, challenges her superstitions, and eventually shows her the practical link between her creative imagination and the way he can help her to manifest it in the real world.

Female Saturn Conjunct Male Neptune. Here the female, through her role of an authoritative "father figure," teaches the male how to focus his imagination. The more he dreams, the more she structures his fantasies. He eventually learns how to constructively crystallize his impressions, his perceptions, and his intuition. This aspect usually occurs to males who have great creative power through imagination but who don't know how to make their dreams manifest. The female becomes the guide, leading her mate to constructive activities; although they may seem to be a bit boring or routine at first, eventually they manifest as "dreams come true." I feel that all great creations are basically one percent inspiration and ninety-nine percent perspiration. This is the karmic lesson the male has to learn if he is able to express his creative power. When his dreams are unrealistic the female stops him, and through a subtle telepathy she teaches him that he is not fulfilling his potential. When his dreams are possible, however, she shows him the kind of results he can achieve just by adding a little effort to the realizations of his sincere fantasies. If the male is success oriented, his partner can help him make it. As she studies his past, she can make him aware of any values he has. She can show him his resources and she can teach him how to channel his creative energies. In essence, she manages him, providing what he needs to reach fulfillment.

There is an unspoken understanding here because of a mystical attunement occurring on an unconscious level. How does the female know everything that her mate needs? Was she important to him in a past incarnation? He will always ask that question. Because she is karmically meant to teach him in this life he will only know the answer when he has earned it.

Male Saturn Conjunct Female Pluto. This aspect symbolizes a karmic ending. The male acts as the desisting force, bringing to a halt the forward momentum of his mate. Thus, she is forced to re-evaluate herself in terms of large constructs. Rather than forging ahead as she was accustomed in the past, she must learn how to thoughtfully ponder the worth of her direction.

Usually this aspect occurs in a relationship when an old karmic lesson is about to be learned. The female's unconscious is being brought to maturity, and she is now able to see the wisdom or repercussions of her past. As a result of this aspect she probably will lose interest in raw sexuality, crude desires, or the baser challenges in life. She will begin to seek that which is of more lasting value. The male uses time to teach his mate the value of life. He shows her that only through the best possible use of time can she begin to focus and manifest all that her unconscious is seeking to express. In time, she will become more practical, rooting out of her consciousness those desires which are ultimately a contradiction to her life's goals, as she learns to focus her energies more productively.

Female Saturn Conjunct Male Pluto. Here the female teaches the male to stop wasting energy and instead, to start expressing the productive goals he truly seeks. Acting through a father-like or authoritarian role, she teaches him the security of pleasing superiors and the fruitlessness of rebelling against his real desires. The relationship often takes on the character of reform achieved through discipline.

The male must karmically end any dissipation through excess sexual energy or crude outlets that don't produce the goals he seeks. His mate actually puts up a "psychic wall" to any destructive energies which might emanate from him, for she only accepts those desires which she can help manifest constructively. The male will have to learn how to stop pushing himself against his own grain. He can begin to look at the long term outcome that his soul is seeking in life, and direct his energies towards the legacy he would like to stand for as his gift for humanity. Where there was dynamic but unchanneled excess energy in the male, there will ultimately be a focused sense of worthiness; not only for himself, but for that special cause or meaning that he would like to dedicate his life to.

Saturn Square Saturn. This aspect creates challenge. Both individuals are tested as each must overcome the obstacles presented by the other before being able to proceed along their karmic path. A tendency to be stubborn and obstinate makes this relationship difficult for both partners. Usually there is some disagreement over an important principle. Through much strife and effort they both must ultimately realize the validity of their own beliefs. Ideological, philosophical, or religious differences may be so powerful that each is shocked by the other. Even so, the relationship is a karmic learning experience through which both partners learn to understand that realities other than their own are perfectly valid.

Male Saturn Square Female Uranus. This aspect reflects a clashing of cultural values. Each individual feels out of his element when dealing with the other on what may appear to be foreign ground. The male symbolizes the customs, tradition, and morality of his ancestral lineage, along with all he has karmically crystallized in past incarnations. The female symbolizes the power for change and all the "decrystallizing" forces that create breaks from conservative ways. He finds her too disruptive; she finds him too stodgy. Both feel discontent as he resists her attempts at pulling him forward.

This aspect usually occurs in relationships which symbolize a choice point in karma. The male, having formed his ways from the past, has reached a level where he has the choice of either bringing all he has formed to fulfillment or changing his direction. He may choose the latter if he doubts the validity of his purpose. Whatever he chooses will be because of the influential effect of the female in this relationship.

Female Saturn Square Male Uranus. The female, often identifying with a father role, is on the verge of outgrowing past obligations. For years (perhaps lifetimes) she attempted to please those in authority. Now she has earned the right to make her own free choices. Through her relationship with the male, she must decide if her future is going to be a continuation along the same path she traveled or if she is going to abandon that path completely and begin a new karma.

The relationship is often filled with strife because so much weighs upon the outcome. The male is felt as a threat to all past traditions that the female tried to stand for. She in turn is seen as limiting his freedom. The more she tries to teach him the value of boundaries, limitations, and rules, the more those ideas lose meaning for her. As a result, she will either rebel against the male's erratic nature and resort to her old ways, or abandon the weight of the past—leaving the excess baggage of her finished karma as she begins a brand new path in life with him.

While she contemplates the significance of this relationship, the male may see her as an obstacle that he must overcome if he is to survive. She symbolizes a wall in his path. And, he too, has decisions to make. He must learn to understand himself amidst the social structure she represents.

This is a powerful aspect for karmic change and personal growth. Both individuals experience one confrontation after another before understanding the important roles they play in each other's lives.

Male Saturn Square Female Neptune. The male looms as an almost insurmountable obstacle that the female must deal with through her imagination. She must find the courage within herself to overcome the barriers he seems to put in her path. He may be discouraged because of her lack of practicality, reasonability, or common sense. Thus, he tries to impose his ideas on her in an effort to force her to conform to his standards. The more he does this, however, the more she feels stifled and cannot express what is flowing through her imaginative processes. She sees his reality as flat and toneless; he sees her reality as having no basis or constructive foundation. He senses her need for discipline, planning, and focus, but he cannot reach her from behind his wall and cannot be true to himself if he comes out in front of it. As a result, a lot of hidden frustration and self-defeatism occur with this aspect. Neither partner is really trying to hurt the other but constant hurts are being inflicted at deep levels. Her compassion has no outlet, yet she may keep trying to find acceptance for it because the male symbolizes the kind of structure that she knows she needs.

This aspect can produce a lackluster marriage with poor communication. It may, nevertheless, continue because each sees a challenge in the other that must be mastered.

Female Saturn Square Male Neptune. The male sees the female as an obstacle to his imagination. She represents something he must overcome in himself if he is to have strength in his beliefs. Yet no matter how powerful the male imagines himself to be, his mate is an insurmountable wall of purpose and meaning for him. She represents authority or an authority figure whose purpose never wavers, regardless of his charm. Therefore, the relationship is one of intense yet subtle challenges that cause both partners to become either secretive or closed. Hidden nuances, unspoken thoughts, intensely piercing glances may take the place of open communication. Ultimately, it is important for both to overcome petty suspicions.

Male Saturn Square Female Pluto. This aspect causes frustration. The female has a turbulent unconscious and must learn to become responsible for her ideas. Her mate issues guidelines which he tries to impose on the relationship. Often his strict traditions, customs, or religious rules are extremely difficult for her to follow. She may feel many youthful impulses while her mate takes on the knowing father role, attempting to teach her countenance, patience, or maturity. Usually this aspect appears in those relationships formed by partners who intimately related in a former life. Because of the growth the female has achieved the relationship forms again in this incarnation so that it can break completely. It is not just the male she needs to break with, but rather the rigid line of reasoning he stands for. When she does make this break it will only be because she has spiritually transcended the rules she once needed.

Female Saturn Square Male Pluto. The female attempts to impose structure, form, and meaning on the male. Her ideas come from others, her past, or a series of father figures whom she respects. The male's understanding comes deep from his unconscious. He rebels against these rules and against the authority that the female is assuming. He will ultimately break from her in order to be responsible for himself.

This aspect symbolizes the continuation of a past-life relationship and it forms again so it can end with understanding. The male must transcend the rules the female is trying to set for him so he can experience his own current. Ultimately, it is not his mate that he is breaking with but rather the idea of bondage. He needs to gain freedom for his own soul.

Saturn Trine Saturn. This aspect brings complementary karmas into a relationship. Both individuals sense a need for cooperatively striving toward goals or objectives. Progress may be slow but steady. An ease of purpose gives both individuals a strong sense of security. This aspect can indicate the kind of harmony which is so hidden it can be taken for granted. It becomes important for both partners to show that they appreciate the worth they see in each other. The value of consistency, easily obtained goals, and a sense of purpose brought about by this aspect should not be overlooked. Two inherently sincere individuals walk on parallel paths confirming each other's direction.

Male Saturn Trine Female Uranus. The male can help to anchor the erratic and adventurous nature of his mate. He adds practicality to her unique ideas and teaches her how to achieve self worth from her inventiveness and ingenuity. She provides the reasons for his rules.

This aspect usually occurs in a relationship where the male is standing for some principle or ethic in life on a karmic level and now needs to impersonalize and free himself from his mission. The female is not part of the central stream of his existence, but because of her impersonal or sometimes apparently meaningless behavior, she frees the male. He needs to be more detached from the principles he stands for or the burdens he carries. She can help him to impersonalize his karma.

Female Saturn Trine Male Uranus. The male acts as a diversion for the overly burdened female. Identifying with the father role, she is often accustomed to carrying responsibilities and being the one who must somehow impose them on those who ignore their commitments. The more she tries to do this with her mate, the more he shakes her loose from her own rigid sense of structure. He can help free her from being too concerned with the central issues in her life, enabling her to deal with them in a more detached manner. She helps provide a framework for his original ideas—she can build, manage and direct his career. There is a mutual understanding of future goals and the way in which they can be attained. This aspect is excellent for material, creative, and scientific advancement as it combines practicality with original ideas.

The female is paying a karmic debt to free herself and she may not often have this kind of a chance. At the same time, the male is receiving the support he has karmically earned.

Male Saturn Trine Female Neptune. The male acts as a buffer for his mate's sensitivities. He effectively grounds her imagination, giving her a foundation in reality that her creative fantasies need. At the same time, she softens his defenses, making it easier for him to express his purpose. This aspect can give powerful meaning and depth to a relationship. The male can see the idealization of his expectations in his mate, for she transcends the boundaries he normally feels. She can teach him how to get beyond his current reality, or how to reach for the dreams that will direct his future. He can learn to sense the colors, tones and nuances upon which he can build a creative lifestyle.

Karmically, he has been concerned with his personal image and she helps him to perceive himself from a different viewpoint. The more he burdens himself with being overly responsible, the more she teaches him how to use his imagination to dissolve the weight of those responsibilities. Through a harmonious blend of knowing what to deal with and what to avoid, this relationship helps both people to find their creative purpose.

Female Saturn Trine Male Neptune. The female leads, guides, and manages her mate by assuming a father role. He has a wide imagination which needs direction if it is to manifest constructively. She is his anchor and while protecting him from the harsh vissicitudes of life, she provides a stable source upon which he can build his hopes and beliefs. Often there is a religious or spiritual connotation here. The male may be in touch with higher essences, he may have a deep intuitive understanding of music or the arts, but he may not know how to express what he feels on a practical level. The female shows him his potential and how meaningful his creative impulses actually are. In turn, he subconsciously idealizes her, using her expectations of him as a set of standards that he must meet.

This aspect releases karmic potential. The male begins to understand his true worth while providing a compassionate and creative outlet for the female's sensitivities. She learns the value of inspirational feeling which ultimately increases her sense of spiritual worth.

Male Saturn Trine Female Pluto. This aspect creates directness. The male provides wisdom and guidance, while his mate offers depth and insight. Great accomplishments can take place through this relationship as both partners sense a need for involvement in something which extends beyond personal needs. The male teaches the female how to direct her energies and she can show him the greater possibilities of all he could reach. As a result each benefits from the strengths of the other.

The female is ending a destructive karma. She learns how to surface and eliminate those thoughts and impulses which are no longer useful because of this relationship and begins to regenerate herself toward more productive ends. In a former incarnation she had rebelled against the forces of limitations and chose a lifestyle outside of the expectations of authority figures. Now she willingly accepts authority and guidance so she can return to a productive and responsible path.

Female Saturn Trine Male Pluto. The female is teaching her mate the value of responsibility by acting a father role. The more he transforms his consciousness, the more he is able to fulfill her expectation of him. At the same time, he shows her the existential possibilities that she can reach if she transcends orthodox thinking.

In a former life the male lost his direction. Through this relationship he now is finding his way back as he accepts the gentle guidance of his partner. She shows him the importance of redirecting sexual energy, as well as the importance of standing for something that is larger than his personal self. She learns how to put into use the principles, form, and structure that she has been saving. Because of this relationship she ends a karma in thought (where she was always the student) and begins a karma in action (as she learns how to teach all she has accumulated).

Saturn Opposite Saturn. This is the most difficult aspect to base a relationship on. Each individual is living out a karma that is in direct opposition to the other. Both partners have conflicting traditions and ways of life that are crystallized. Past habit patterns and methods of dealing with life are challenged in this relationship as each begins to see the validity of the other but cannot follow the path of the opposition.

This aspect occurs in partnerships when a fourteen year difference in age occurs. Socio-economic and cultural difference exist due to a generational time lag in which history tends to repeat itself. The older partner may try to recreate the past, while the younger partner is trying to meet the expectations of the future. Both individuals are concerned with a practical reality but neither one can feel it in this relationship. Two powerful and heavily laden ships pass in the night, both bound for different destinations.

Male Saturn Opposite Female Uranus. The male tries to possessively control the erratic female. Her sense of freedom and originality is a threat to the security he expects to find with her. Acting the role of his father, he may discover that the methods which bound his consciousness in the past do little to affect his most impersonal mate. He slowly begins to free himself from the burden of the tradition he has been carrying. In doing so he must break from everything that made him feel secure. This becomes an extremely difficult aspect for the male. His partner tests him again and again to see if what he stands for actually has real meaning for him.

This aspect occurs in relationships which are learning experiences. The male, after having long followed a certain line of reason, sees reason to oppose his own path, yet he is not quite ready to assume the responsibility for thinking in such a manner. Nevertheless, his unconscious need for acceptance magnetizes this original thinking and free spirited female into his life. Through her initiative he will begin breaking old habits and learn how to accept the freedom that she is teaching him to experience.

Since the female is literally shaking the male from his roots she experiences much obstinacy and frustration, yet she cannot really possess him for herself. This aspect produces a change in a karmic pattern which is particularly difficult for the male. It does not have the ingredients necessary for a harmonious enduring partnership or marriage. But it does free the male, making him more ready for a more fulfilling relationship in the future.

Female Saturn Opposite Male Uranus. The female is confronted with an attraction to a male from a walk of life that is completely different than her own. She is going against the traditions of her father, her ancestral lineage and in some cases even her spiritual background. Although this can be extremely difficult for her, the male represents a freedom from the past that she has been seeking but could not obtain by herself. She needs him to symbolize what she cannot yet express.

There is much torment here for the relationship tears her from her roots and forces her to establish new foundations. As a result of an unfinished karmic relationship in a past incarnation, the male's appearance on the scene is more important to her than the security she has built for herself in this life. The strain of the relationship will test that security, as well as her other values, until she makes a choice between a desire to preserve her past or a need to reach for the excitement of an uncertain future. If she reaches for the future, the relationship is likely to break; for the male is in her life for the sole purpose of freeing her. If she stays rooted to her family, the relationship will probably continue because it offers a challenge to the male that he must accept. Nevertheless, the female will be frustrated.

The greatest difficulty may result because the male is viewed as being unsteady, erratic, or inconstant by her family and friends. He becomes the crusader who is fighting for the freedom of a damsel he will never have.

Male Saturn Opposite Female Neptune. This aspect often symbolizes unrequited love. The male is attached to the traditions and station in life upon which his character is built. If he reaches for the female, he loses the importance of his own identity. She symbolizes his unattainable dream and gives to him the colorful impressions that add feeling and depth to his being. Still, he cannot detach from his karmic mission in life, and a powerful attraction causes frustration.
unable to find lasting fulfillment.

The female dreams of her mate and imagines the most wonderful things for him. She tries to soften his defenses and somehow permeates his tough exterior personality through osmosis. In fact, she does reach him in many ways, but his inability to understand her subtleties makes it almost impossible for him to know this. Instead he may put up one barrier after another in order to prevent himself from surrendering to his heart's desire.

This relationship brings out the conflict between form and no form, structure and no structure, tradition and wandering. As a result of karmic separation in a past life, both individuals meet now in an attempt to fulfill what their souls have been missing. Because time and experience has come between them, each is following a different path in life. The male has learned how to build his security through a permanent structuring of ideas. The female has identified with sorrow. Although both have much to give each other, there is too much of a gap between their identification systems for this relationship to run smoothly. The male tries to set the example for his partner to follow and she cannot meet his expectations.

Female Saturn Opposite Male Neptune. The female tries to teach the male the values of responsibility by acting a father role. She sees him as an escapist, slipping away from the burdens of life. In a past incarnation, there was an unfinished bond which brings both individuals together now. The female tries to secure the relationship through structure, form, and the building of realistic foundations. Because she is more secure than the male, this structure has more meaning for her than it does for him. He values the lessons she offers, but cannot realize the full import as she intends it. Instead his dreams may take him in and out of the partnership.

There is much frustration here as the female cannot have herself and the male also. The more she tries to hold him, the more she loses her solid identification in reality. Ultimately she must make a decision between having her mate and fulfilling her mission to herself. She is the sands of time. He is the wave beating against the shoreline. Each takes from the other as these two powerful forces meet.

Male Saturn Opposite Female Pluto. This aspect produces a hectic but dynamic relationship. The male tries to teach the female how to follow an ultimately productive path. She tries to transcend the limitations that he values. There are cultural differences here and they tend to become magnified. Each individual sees the force of society in a different way. The male understands how his growth will occur through abiding in traditional and socially acceptable customs. The female sees the progress in society as occurring through revolutionary transformations which often topple the conservative forces of tradition. Thus, each has their own powerfully ingrained values.

The male is karmically testing his strength as he learns the ways to suppress and keep the undercurrent of destructive forces that he feels in his mate in check. At the same time, she is testing the values of traditional rules in an attempt to find her own unique identity. Much challenge occurs as both partners feel there is more at stake than just winning over the other. Each will generalize the attitudes learned in this relationship toward many other people in life.

Due to the two strong forces that oppose each other, the relationship takes on the nuance of desisting and stilling all that had been set in progress before. During this time, both reassess and re-evaluate all they stand for in order to make important decisions about the future direction of their lives. The outcome of this partnership often involves the female breaking family ties and searching deep into herself to find her very reason for existence. At the same time, the male is meeting his most difficult challenge. All he has ever held as being secure will be shaken to the very core, with only the seed of substantial truth remaining.

Female Saturn Opposite Male Pluto. The female acts the role of father and is the subjugating force over the male. She represents power that he is trying to transcend. There can be much torment here for she often finds herself standing for much more than she wants to in an effort to maintain structure and form in what would otherwise be an extremely insecure relationship.

She uses the rules she was taught in order to teach the male how to focus his dynamic energies. He not only questions her authority but goes to the core of her tradition to see if he can find loopholes in reason, flaws in logic, or decadence in what he might be able to replace. As a result, the relationship symbolizes a powerful challenge for both individuals. The difficulty is more than a personal one. Both partners are questioning the validity of long-ingrained thoughts which have wide reaching effects. The female has valued those limiting forces in society which help to maintain structure, form and order, while the male symbolizes the revolutionary and regenerative forces which try to transcend established customs. The relationship has powerful philosophic and attitudinal overtones for both partners. Two successful adversaries stand glaring at each other, each realizing that he has met his match.

This is one of the few aspects that can contain past life hate, mistrust, and an "enemy-like" consciousness. Whether or not both individuals actually knew each other is less important than how powerfully each stands for what the other detests. Ultimately, through a series of powerful clashes, each will resolve the karma by more clearly understanding his own meaning.

Uranus Aspects

Uranus Conjunct Uranus. This aspect creates a great deal of electricity. Both individuals share an intense interest in life and are able to stimulate each other intellectually. There is a ready flow of ideas, discoveries, and learning as each partner values the open-mindedness of the other. The relationship will have many unexpected changes, but because of them both individuals will experience a great deal of growth and awareness.

Male Uranus Conjunct Female Neptune. The female inspires the intellect of her mate. She adds intuition and feeling to his understandings. He sparks her imagination, adding vividness and a sense of progress to her life. There can be great spiritual illumination here, as both partners function through the impersonal aspects of themselves and become aware of a greater reality. ESP and the psychic centers connect to establish strong telepathic wavelengths. As a result, a learning experience is exchanged on levels higher than verbal communication.

Female Uranus Conjunct Male Neptune. The female brightens the dreams of her mate. She intensifies his belief system and makes him aware of the correctness of his impressions. As a result, she can help him confirm a reality he is only vaguely in touch with. Through ESP both partners experience heightened states of consciousness. The male adds feeling and intuitiveness to the female's intellect. It is important for both partners to keep their feet firmly rooted on the ground, for as each helps the other to expand consciousness there are many thoughts, ideas and impressions that must be checked against the backdrop of reality.

Male Uranus Conjunct Female Pluto. This aspect creates a dynamic transforming quality in a relationship. The higher intellectual awareness of the male combines with the depth of the female to provide new and often startling realizations about life. There is inventiveness, discovery, progress and much evolution. But the partnership is not peaceful. Because of many changes in sexual attitude, the female throws away the waste matter of her past as her mate points the way to the future. This process involves turmoil for her karmic darkness can fight the enlightenment it needs to receive. In the end, a sense of immediacy along with the understanding of how to live in the present become the tone of this relationship.

Female Uranus Conjunct Male Pluto. The female brings light, inspiration, and futuristic vision to her transforming mate. He is coming out of darkness and because of his relationship with her, he sees the reality of a world filled with freshness, newness, and discovery. At the same time, she receives his ideas about transformation. Many sexual changes create one turbulent transformation after another and the partnership spirals its way upward in consciousness as both partners realize their true potential in the Now.*

Uranus Square Uranus. This is an extremely difficult aspect for a relationship. It creates impatience, intolerance, and a heightened sense of individualism in both partners. As a result, too much frustration and antagonism can occur as each person tries to assert free will. Both have something to teach but each would rather learn through personal experience rather than at the advice of another. As a result irritating challenges arise and can cause breaks and separations. Difficulty can also stem from too much excitement in too many areas. Both partners see so many existential possibilities they want to experience that it becomes almost unnatural for them to experience a comfortable settled feeling in each other. A match lights a match which lights a match which lights a match . . . .

Male Uranus Square Female Neptune. This aspect causes poor judgment. The female's impressions, dreams, and illusions tend to cloud the intellect of the male. In turn, he overreacts and often misses the point. She finds it difficult to trust her intuitive self because his unpredictable excitability often disrupts her stream of consciousness. Thus, this relationship puts a strain on both partners. The male, being more impersonal than his mate, tends to feel less of the hurt that each is inadvertently inflicting on the other. Dreams go unrealized. Future expectations do not materialize. Both partners in an attempt not to blame the other tend to unconsciously become isolated. A sense of incompleteness becomes the tone for the relationship.

Female Uranus Square Male Neptune. The female may experience a lot of self doubt. She may receive incorrect impressions from her mate. The more she tries to understand

*See *Karmic Astrology, Volume IV—The Karma of The Now,* by Martin Schulman, Samuel Weiser, Inc., York Beach, ME, 1979.

him, the more she grows confused for his vague and intuitive patterns seem to keep eluding definition. She is restless, desiring to activate his dreams, but because she doesn't really understand what they are she tends to be caught in a cross current of uneasy confusion. The male tries to please his partner even though she misunderstands his most endearing efforts.

Male Uranus Square Female Pluto. This is a powerful and volatile aspect. Suspicions arise because behavior is awkward and subversive. The male seeks to find what the female is hiding from him for he senses a covert attitude that keeps eluding his understanding. He probes and searches, trying to catch his mate by surprise in the hope that somehow he will unlock her unconscious secrets. Both partners are highly individualistic and because of this, the relationship ultimately becomes a struggle for survival. There can be obsession here, often occurring as a result of frustrated passions. If the partnership is to work, both individuals must recognize each other's private individuality while also understanding that outlooks on life can be different without necessarily being better or worse.

Female Uranus Square Male Pluto. A lack of trust is the dominant tone of the relationship. The female tries to enlighten her mate and keeps crashing into his unconscious. His resentment causes more rebelliousness in her. The ways in which he retaliates are often under the surface and quite subtle. Thus, each partner can get caught up in a suspicious struggle for power. As a result, this aspect causes intense difficulties for even extremely sophisticated individuals. The higher the degree of evolution, the more expansive and disproportionate can be the struggles. Individual principles take precedence when one is involved in elemental karma, but cultural or universal principles still exist when one is in a more evolved karma. As a result, two individuals can experience great difficulty in achieving harmony.

When the female tries to relate to a male through her impersonal self (Uranus), it is often a cause in the world that prompts her spirit. In essence, she may struggle to pry open his hidden conceptions of mass consciousness in an attempt to revolutionize and change the dormant potential that she sees. In effect, it is the world she is trying to change in order to get to the male who is hiding behind it.

Uranus Trine Uranus. This aspect stimulates intellectual exploration. Both partners cooperatively feel the need to seek, discover, and use the innovative power of their minds. Each admires the originality and uniqueness in the other; each tends to see the relationship as having a very special freeing quality. The more each feels closer to the other, the more freedom of self is experienced. Rather than this being a binding aspect, it becomes a harmonious source of interests and ideals whose complementary relationship with each other can create more meaningful yet intangible bonds. Each partner helps enlighten the other as both discover that their greatest interest is based on a common need to give to and share in mankind's evolution.

Male Uranus Trine Female Neptune. The male intellect adds interest and opportunity to her imagination; he helps her free her dreams, casting off the shackles of unconscious inhibitions and helping her focus her mind. At the same time, she adds color, depth, and tone to all he is capable of understanding. Much spiritual growth can take place through expanded states of consciousness because each partner helps to stimulate the other. The male is free and independent; his mate is romantic and imaginative. The learning and growth that occur are natural and easy.

Female Uranus Trine Male Neptune. The female stimulates her mate's dreams. The more he inspires her intellect, the more she discovers new ideas for his imagination to color. Intuitive and intellectual ease allow both partners to experience a free-flowing stream of consciousness. The relationship fosters a reservoir of unexpected creativity which spirals both individuals to higher levels of awareness. All activities sparked by inspiration from the creative imagination can become a source of fascination for both partners.

Male Uranus Trine Female Pluto. The inventive and original male qualities blend with the regenerative forces in the female to produce changes, transformations and evolutionary growth. The male provides intellectual curiosity and the female searches for the answers to life at the very bottom of her soul. Together both partners experience a harmonious quest in search of discovering the unknown. They seek, through common interests, to discover the existential potential of mankind.

Female Uranus Trine Male Pluto. The female finds reason to use her scientific and investigative inquisitiveness because her mate provides the depth which sparks the search. She adds interest, intellectual stimulation, and the existential tolerance which give the relationship scope and potential. Both partners will be somewhat individualistic, but can share a common outlook as well as a common interest in helping to transform the state of mankind.

Uranus Opposite Uranus. This is a rare aspect to find in a relationship because a forty-two year difference exists. In addition to the chronological and maturity problems signified by this age difference, the aspect itself symbolizes opposing idealistic outlooks. There may be disagreements regarding matters of free will or the direction in which original thinking should lead the relationship, as well as a disparity between each partner's orientation with the existing culture. This aspect may cause a great deal of frustration, intolerance or misunderstandings as both male and female are opposed in what the other believes is their role in society. Controversy stimulates growth, however, for disagreements can be the very root of a learning experience. And difficulties are the very real stepping stones upon which individuality is ultimately built. The challenges in this relationship could be a testing ground for the spiritual evolution of each partner.

Male Uranus Opposite Female Neptune. This aspect can cause conflicts in objectives. The male seeks to discover, originate, and reach for goals and ideals which symbolize his future. His mate tends to drift and the more she fantasizes, the more difficult it becomes for her partner to communicate with her. He may become frustrated because her seemingly aimless wandering thwarts his sense of progress and dampens his excitement. Spiritual realizations can be monumental but the ability to put them into practice in this relationship is exceedingly difficult.

Female Uranus Opposite Male Neptune. The female attempts to stimulate her mate's imagination because she sees the vivid possibilities of his dreams. However, when she tries to activate these fantasies into reality, she finds that a basic conflict in the relationship prevents her from doing so. The male has a sense of non-desire akin to passively accepting life as the scenery which rules his mind. She tries to bring him to enlightenment, but the awareness she has to offer may be difficult for him to believe or accept. Her active striving toward the realization of future goals is viewed passively, almost as a spectator watches a scene without participating in it.

Male Uranus Opposite Female Pluto. This is an extremely difficult aspect. Both partners are highly individualistic and strong willed. Both have powerful opinions, ideas, and attitudes. Both know how to achieve their goals but both view life from two different extremes. The male favors the immediacy of change, while his mate strives to bring about the slower, more permanent changes which result in complete transformations. Through one challenge after another, each partner tries to assert the truth of their beliefs. The rabbit races the turtle, but neither knows the reason for the race or the reward for the winner.

Female Uranus Opposite Male Pluto. The female attempts to understand the depths in her mate. Her lack of patience and tolerance urges her on to seek immediate answers rather than stepping back to see the entire picture. She may see parts of the transformation that the male experiences through her, but rarely the totality.

Both partners are seeking a karmic change. The female impatiently strives for the immediate improvements that will satisfy her impersonal ideals for mankind. The male seeks to transform those deep undercurrents in life, which ultimately change the shape of mankind's destiny. Since both partners are striving for individualistic evolutionary ideas, discovering new ways and lifestyles, and finding some unknown quality that represents humanistic reform, the relationship has much dynamic conflict that it must progress through. Great material and spiritual achievements may take place if each partner can see the value or the importance of what they can give to humanity.

Neptune Aspects

Neptune Conjunct Neptune. This aspect is found as a reflection of generational beliefs and feelings. Both partners are receptive to the same qualities in life. We have a strong telepathic or psychic link with people born close in time. Since beliefs are so intangible, one never knows for sure if they are valid. However, this aspect allows an individual to confirm or validate his beliefs with another.

Sometimes our generation's beliefs and impressions take a spiritual course. They may reflect a trend that is appearing and dissolving within the more fixed framework of the total culture that is being experienced through the aspect.

Neptune Square Neptune. This aspect is often found in mentor or student-teacher relationships in which each person attempts to envision their ideals in the other. There is a large age difference here which puts strain on the relationship and sometimes makes communication difficult. The younger individual sees the dreams of his future in the Neptune square, while the older individual sees the youth capable of realizing all he imagines.

Because this aspect is so subtle, it takes many years for both partners to realize what they have learned from each other. This can be a very important experience for the younger individual. The older individual can perceive the ways in which the world has changed since he formed his own impressions of reality.

There is a timeless quality here. Both individuals are able to understand the qualities of the imagination which transcend age or generational changes. However, each must let go of stereotyped opinions that they learned through their peers. In essence, both individuals try to prove the validity of their own place in time, each wanting the other to accept their ideals.

Neptune Trine Neptune. This aspect has been omitted as it seldom occurs in a relationship.

Neptune Opposite Neptune. This aspect has been omitted as it seldom occurs in a relationship.

Pluto Aspects

Pluto Conjunct Pluto. This aspect is generational as most relationships will have it. Both partners will be pressured by similar unconscious desires which reflect both their age and place in history. Thoughts and ideas may be measured in terms of their ultimate worth in relation to the greater scheme of things. The essential purpose in life is an important undercurrent in this partnership.

Pluto Square, Trine or Opposite Pluto. These aspects have been omitted as they seldom occur between partners in a personal relationship.

HOROSCOPE DELINEATION

The nature of a relationship is always multi-faceted. There will always be areas of agreement and discord which create an intermingling of different levels of understanding. One should never hope to oversimplify the complex ties because many overt and covert or clear and subtle nuances take place when two individuals attempt to relate to each other. It becomes important to understand each facet on several levels—first, in and of itself; secondly, how this facet relates to other parts of one's being; and finally, how much or how little a facet of a relationship affects the total picture.

While some aspects are decidedly more difficult than others, the outcome of a relationship or marriage can never be based on one aspect alone. Individuals may have sexual difficulties (which may or may not be ironed out) that may ultimately be less important than their philosophical or emotional outlook. In other instances, sexual difficulties may be so pronounced that they interfere with a smooth flow of consciousness on other levels. The astrologer should study all the indications so that the aspects can be categorized by strength or weakness. The aspects symbolizing difficulties or karmic problems should also be considered. In this last area, the karmic problems, comes the most difficult decisions, for here the astrologer must determine how far any problem solving will take an individual away from himself.

The goal of understanding the nature of a relationship is to eventually create more harmony in it. The astrologer can point out the advantages and disadvantages of the different aspects, leaving it to the clients to find the personal methods of dealing with what they can live with, or choosing not to deal with what they can't.

It is interesting to note that problems in the relationship already exist in most instances where a relationship reading is desired. People seldom come to astrologers with questions about relationships that are working smoothly. They have many questions when something in a partnership is either confusing, perplexing, or draining them of any hope for an optimistic future. Sometimes this is nothing more than self doubt, amplified because of each partner's inability to inspire confidence in the other. Where self doubt exists, the astrologer can point it out; otherwise it could easily create a weak spot in the relationship, making future problems or obstacles difficult to overcome.

Sometimes positive (constructive) traits in relationships are clouded because too much attention is being paid to minor difficulties. Many people have difficulty accepting or even understanding true love. They often find it easier to display false personalities than to admit to the goodness that is possible if they take a chance and open up. People sometimes have opinions about their relationships that may not accurately reflect the true nature of what they are experiencing. Problems and obstacles exist for a reason. They can be the stepping stones of spiritual growth; in effect, problems can create a stairway to enlightenment. Yet objectivity is easily clouded by the desires and attitudes of the subjective unconscious. As a result, feelings, trends, and even a sense of direction can become difficult to comprehend when looked for too closely. The astrologer can counsel objectivity when a client is interpreting the effect of aspects felt subjectively.

Love is a healer. It smooths over the inconsistencies in life, warming one's feelings, and enabling one to see that ultimately a sense of harmony with oneself and the person one loves is the true objective in life. Sometimes, we do things for others because we love them. But, in doing so, we can overstep our bounds trying to achieve for another that which we think is good for that person rather than allowing the partner to grow according to personal needs.

It becomes important to try to objectively detach ourselves when we study our relationships. This way, we can get a clearer picture of what is actually taking place. In some instances, two individuals can feel great love for each other even though a karmic condition indicates a basic incompatibility. Sometimes, two people don't love each other at all, but can get along easily because of an ability to share a similar karmic pathway. This, too, must enter into the final analysis; for there is always a reason why a relationship exists.

The single most important factor to keep in mind when trying to understand a relationship is the sad fact that people lie. People lie to themselves, to relatives and friends, to spouse or lover, and often, even to their God! They often see themselves, as well as the relationship they are in, through the muddled haze of dreams and expectations. They want a particular partnership or marriage to work or not work. They read into it whatever their imagination will tolerate. Unable to face themselves, they may place blame on the people nearest to them; they may be unable to relate on a realistic basis or they may exalt those they love and put them on some imaginary cloud or pedestal. These people can both blame and exalt lovers, using their imagination as the basis of all reason.

Thus, consciously or unconsciously, with intent or quite inadvertently, people color the truth. But astrology does not distort. It clearly shows the forces working in a relationship as they are. This puts a certain responsibility on astrologers, for in their love for people, they may sometimes find themselves believing the distortions heard from the client. Astrologers, then, must be careful not to become involved emotionally in the outcome of any relationship. Instead, astrologers must *believe* the charts. Unfortunately, charts are only pieces of paper with symbols on them—they do not have the power to smile warmly or act sadly when confronted with certain realizations—so clients can easily evoke astrologers' sympathies. The greatest service we can perform is to help an individual see his true path. If astrologers are as objective as possible, they will ultimately provide what the client needs. In fact, when an individual has questions about a relationship, astrologers can go much deeper; often revealing answers to questions the client never thought of asking. In order to do this it is important to study the total essence of a relationship rather than addressing only the specific question that the client asks.

In order to better understand the interpretation and synthesis of the aspects I have described, I would like to refer the reader to the following famous couple. Everyone knows that one of the most public and fascinating relationships was the long and stormy love between Richard Burton and Elizabeth Taylor. Newspaper accounts of their private lives, while to some extent glamorized or clouded, tend to reveal little about the inner workings of this relationship. The charts, however, show many aspects and ties. In order to obtain a clear picture of the relationship, discard the rumors, newspaper accounts and the effect of publicity releases for the moment. In this way, we can understand the relationship as the product of two very real individuals, not unlike ourselves, but nevertheless unique in terms of their horoscopes. Their charts are reproduced on pages 134 and 135. For the reader's convenience, a list of aspects appears on page 136.

Elizabeth Taylor—Richard Burton

In Elizabeth Taylor's chart, her Scorpio Moon conjuncts Burton's Sun. This is one of the most constructive aspects for a fulfilling marriage. It shows that the female is capable of nourishing her mate, while his strength ultimately becomes a powerful central focus in her life. Quite literally, the female becomes the reflection of all the male emanates. She may wrap her life around him, while his brilliance and strength become her source of inspiration.

Taylor's Scorpio Moon, however, forms two other aspects which modify this basic magnetism. It trines Burton's retrograde Uranus in Pisces which on the one hand adds a note of exhilaration and excitement to the relationship, but on the other, loosens the closeness of the Sun-Moon conjunction. The female, through a mothering role, helps the male to break away from his mother. She may be forced to balance the close dependency of the Sun-Moon conjunction relationship with the possible freedom that the Moon trine Uranus aspect demands. Her Moon placement would indicate an intense emotional response that would have to be both possessive and detached; a difficulty dichotomy to balance.

With her Scorpio Moon also forming a square to his Neptune in Leo, another modification enters the emotional relationship. She may experience an unconscious loneliness similar to something her mother felt as her idealized conception of Burton keeps dissolving. The more she identifies with him in order to better understand him, the more she may lose touch with herself. When he seeks comfort and mothering, she may unconsciously resent the symbolic re-enactment of the childhood he is trying to escape from. There may follow misunderstandings, a lack of clear intentions, and some identity confusion that makes it difficult for both individuals to define where they stand in the relationship.

In the chart of Richard Burton, we find Sun in Scorpio forming a trine to Taylor's Sun in Pisces. This is an excellent aspect for marriage as it can indicate similar paths in life. Both individuals are capable of sharing experiences with each other because outlook and attitude enhance the creative spirit. Burton's Sun forms a trine to her Mercury in Pisces as well. This aspect indicates he can show her the greatness of her ideas as well as help her to express power and brilliance, through communication. Both of these trines indicate that the relationship would inspire Burton's own feelings of brilliance, exaltation and importance. The Sun-Sun trine, however, is colored by some competitiveness indicated as a result of influences which are external to the relationship.

Her Sun forms four aspects to Burton's chart. It trines his Saturn in Scorpio creating purpose, guidelines and ultimate goals that both partners would support in order to achieve a sense of station in life. The female can function optimistically within the parameters of her mate, helping the relationship

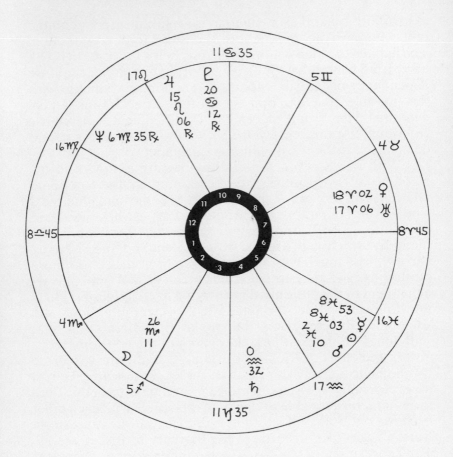

Elizabeth Taylor's chart. She was born February 27, 1932, in London, England. Data obtained from *An Astrological Who's Who* by Marc Penfield, Arcane Books, York Harbor, Maine, 1972, p. 447.

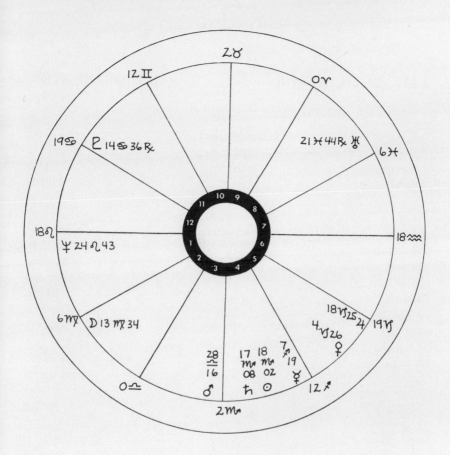

Richard Burton's chart. He was born November 10, 1925, in
Pontrhydyfen, Wales. Data obtained from *An Astrological
Who's Who* by Marc Penfield, Arcane Books, York Harbor,
Maine, 1971, p. 64.

THE ASPECTS

ELIZABETH TAYLOR		RICHARD BURTON
Moon	conjunct	Sun
Jupiter	conjunct	Neptune
Neptune	conjunct	Moon
Pluto	conjunct	Pluto
Sun	square	Mercury
Moon	square	Neptune
Mercury	square	Mercury
Venus	square	Jupiter
Mars	square	Mercury
Saturn	square	Mars
Uranus	square	Jupiter
Jupiter	square	Saturn
Sun	trine	Sun
Sun	trine	Saturn
Sun	trine	Pluto
Moon	trine	Uranus
Mercury	trine	Sun
Mercury	trine	Saturn
Mercury	trine	Pluto
Venus	trine	Neptune
Mars	trine	Mars
Jupiter	trine	Mercury
Uranus	trine	Neptune
Neptune	trine	Venus
Pluto	trine	Uranus
Sun	opposite	Moon
Mercury	opposite	Moon
Mars	opposite	Neptune
Pluto	opposite	Jupiter

build stature and the accumulation of material wealth. Both share a sense of "giantism" as their lives are building something that will long outlast them.

These qualities are somewhat altered because hard aspects to her Sun would make her feel that the marriage was somehow cheating her of the fulfillment she desires. Her Sun in Pisces forms a square to his Mercury in Sagittarius causing a frustration or a fear of not fulfilling his expectations. This aspect works better in a platonic friendship or business partnership or any relationship that does not involve sexuality. In a marriage, however, the male's conscious thoughts struggle to overcome his mate's dominant image. This difficulty is magnified further because Taylor's Sun forms an opposition to his Moon. He may try to overcome a mother image by opposing himself to his mate. He must recognize the power of the female if he is to achieve this freedom. He may also unconsciously resent the feelings of ignominity and helplessness that this aspect can engender. The affliction to his Moon can make him feel like a reflection of what he should be. A re-enactment of childhood memories, confrontations with his wife, and because of his perception of his own image, this relationship may make him feel cheated— for he may not want to deal with the unconscious stirrings that this aspect causes.

It is interesting to note how the Sun-Moon conjunction (his Sun, her Moon) would bring these people so close and yet the Sun-Moon opposition (her Sun, his Moon) would make them feel so far apart at the same time. The trine between her Sun in Pisces and his Pluto in Cancer shows the fascinating dichotomy between darkness and light that literally dazzled the public. The relationship could regenerate through this aspect, as her creative brilliance becomes more powerful when it is triggered by his Plutonic energy. There is a dynamic quality that pours from this and any disagreements between the partners would probably only enhance their powerful external influence on the world. The raw qualities of the male are necessary for the transformation of the female. At the same time, the more he realizes the need for her light, the more he inadvertently brings himself to truth.

Burton's Moon in Virgo forms an opposition to her Mercury in Pisces. This aspect causes a contradiction between his feelings and her ideas. He senses a lack in her protective instinct and may try to make her communicate her feelings. If she tries to do this only to please him, she can develop an inner resentment about being taught how to be "motherly." This aspect can lead to frustration, discontent and may even ultimately prove to be the disruptive element in the relationship. Since Burton's Moon forms a conjunction to Taylor's Neptune, some of this energy softens because of a powerful and sensitive psychic and emotional attraction. Both individuals are more in tune with each other than their verbal communication might indicate. But their closeness is intangible. It is a form of soul contact which loses much of its flow when it is put into words. Each is unconsciously receptive to the moods and feelings of the other, yet on conscious levels, the Moon-Mercury opposition may make it difficult to realize.

We can see that thirteen Sun and Moon aspects show that this relationship has both powerful strengths and disappointing weaknesses. The female is a strong central image and is more dominant in this relationship because there are four aspects to her Sun. The male is forced in turn to cope with challenges where he symbolically acts out unconscious childhood feelings about his own mother (three aspects to Burton's Moon). He also must deal with his impression of what "woman" as a symbol (in an impersonal sense) is to him.

The conjunction between Jupiter (in Taylor's chart) and Neptune (in Burton's chart) shows a higher spiritual force working through their relationship. Wisdom and the higher mind combine with intuition to produce a more cosmic understanding of life. There may be a sense of universal destiny; a longing for that which is beyond the next unseen horizon, a mystical union that includes generosity and compassion that may extend beyond personal levels. With Pluto conjunct Pluto, each individual feels a need to transform something. Through these two conjunctions, a transcendental tone is set in this relationship and both partners may experience understandings which move through the channels of time and space as if perpetuated by a continuum of its own. Because of these aspects the world has wondered about the kind of lifestyle and consciousness Elizabeth Taylor and Richard Burton experienced together. The Jupiter-Neptune conjunction never really touches earth, but instead tends to create a larger-than-life fantasy in which both individuals attempt to seek their cosmic meaning. Experiencing higher understandings of reality, or even the exaggerations of fantasy, are rarely enough to compensate for frustrations on mundane levels. Richard Burton is an actor of noteworthy quality. His Mercury (the planet of communication) forms a square to Elizabeth Taylor's Sun and he undoubtedly felt somewhat overshadowed by her light. This aspect often produces a kind of nervous irritability which makes it difficult for either partner to discover personal inner virtues or talents. The Mercurial individual (in this case Burton) might inadvertently become resentful because he has to work at communicating himself while the Sun individual doesn't have to do anything but "shine." A personal sense of inadequacy arising from the Mercury square makes it difficult to compete with, or even impress, the dazzling brilliance of the Sun. These frustrations would be heightened even more because of the Mercury square Mercury aspect. Both partners are interested in the communicative arts; both partners earn a living and receive meaning from the life work through the power of the spoken word. The square creates tension with little constructive result. While either partner could be successful in and of themselves, the ability to communicate a meaning in life to the other would be a constant source of strife. Even their views and ideas of how the other should communicate would be in discord.

Elizabeth Taylor's Jupiter forms a trine to Richard Burton's Mercury, indicating that in the midst of these difficulties in communication, she could use her higher mind to understand the essence of what her mate was trying to express. But here too, Burton would feel at a disadvantage. Depending on her to understand what he means causes even more frustration. She could expand his ideas and see a philosophical value in them, but could he do it himself? To balance this feeling of inadequacy, he would have to resort to his Saturn energy—which forms a trine to her Mercury. He could draw wisdom from past tradition, showing her the profoundness of her ideas as well as encouraging her. Through

Jupiter, Taylor brings out the lightness, and the higher understanding, and through his Saturn, Burton brings out the purpose, meaning and ultimate value of shared ideas. Jupiter and Saturn tend to have opposite effects. Where Jupiter expands, Saturn contracts. Where Jupiter uplifts, Saturn turns toward the more restrictive path. Where Jupiter reaches for the future, Saturn keeps building on the past. When these two planets are working harmoniously with each other, they produce an expansive spectrum through time and both individuals experience a rather wide perspective on life. There is no question that this was true in the Burton-Taylor relationship. With four afflictions to Mercury, these two trines (Jupiter trine Mercury and Saturn trine Mercury) had to bear the brunt of balancing the most important area in their lives—their ability to communicate. Some of the lightness that one might expect to find in a trine is exhausted prematurely because the individuals become too reliant on this energy to compensate for more difficult areas in their lives.

A more positive trine is found between Venus and Neptune. In fact, this trine also appears in reverse. Thus Taylor's Venus forms a trine to Burton's Neptune while his Venus forms a trine to hers. This is the glamour aspect. It creates a mystical quality of intrigue and fantasy that can become an aura around the couple. Both enjoy similar tastes in music and there is a harmonious blending of feelings. This is where the astute astrologer must clearly distinguish between emotions and feelings. The Taylor-Burton relationship shows much emotional discord because of the different Moon afflictions but, aside from only one affliction to Venus, there is a basic harmony of feeling.

Emotions are the outer coverings of feelings. Emotions change as the weather changes, as circumstances in life change, as day to day conditions change. But feeling is usually more stable. An individual can argue with another because of emotions while still retaining great love, admiration, and respect for that person because of feeling.

We can see how the afflictions to the Moon indicate one thing, while the harmonious aspects to Venus can show quite another. The Burton-Taylor relationship would have its stormy moments, but through it all there would have been an overriding "feeling" that each individual had for the other. Unfortunately, the square between Taylor's Venus and Burton's Jupiter would present a serious block to the free flowing of feeling that existed in the relationship. This aspect may cause insecurity on the woman's part. She waits to receive her love and may find that his expansive nature seeks more from life than a one-to-one relationship. When she tries to offer affection, his identification with philosophical attitudes, proverbs, and distant ideas may be a constant source of irritation to her. Misunderstanding her intentions, he can try to impress her with knowledge or noble and chivalrous attitudes rather than giving her the love and affection she is looking for. If the male is willing to abdicate the throne of his understanding, then he can begin to feel all she is trying to tell him. Difficulties occur in this relationship—not out of a lack of love or genuine feeling—but rather because of who each is. Burton admires philosophy and the wisdom of the ancients. Taylor is more a product of woman's archetypal romantic nature. This conflict between Jupiter and Venus reflects the age-old dilemma of the Greek philosopher, caught between the value of his ideas and the woman he loves; while she in turn must go through his philosophy in order to reach him. A sense of distance is created causing invisible barriers that make it difficult for love to prosper.

With Elizabeth Taylor's Venus and Uranus both forming squares to Burton's Jupiter, an eccentric sense of extravagance might prevail in the relationship. Overly large (Jupiter) and unique (Uranus) gifts or presents (Jupiter-Venus) might take the place of developing the ability to communicate. Yet if one assumes that this relationship contains overwhelming difficulties, remember that there are thirteen trine aspects indicating many areas of harmony, cooperation and spiritual growth.

The trine from Taylor's Mercury to Burton's Pluto indicates a very deep understanding. The female communicates with the well of her passion and mystery in the male, while he provides the unceasing generation of power from the depths of his soul which can help her transform her consciousness. This aspect helps her find it easier to transcend her fears and self doubts. But this is not a one-sided experience because Burton's Uranus forms a trine to her Pluto. Thus she also provides depth for him, helping his intellectual search to be validated by her quest for answers deep within her soul. Through common interest both partners seek to discover the existential potential of mankind.

In the Uranus-Neptune trine, we see the way the female (Uranus) stimulates the dreams of her mate (Neptune). The more he inspires her intellect, the more she discovers new ideas for his imagination to color. Intuitive and intellectual ease allow both partners to experience a free-flowing stream of consciousness. The relationship fosters creativity that can spiral both partners to higher levels of awareness. This is a generosity aspect. It brings about constructive and compassionate understanding while heightening intuitive communication.

Perhaps some of the greatest difficulties in this relationship stem from a confusion in roles. There are three Mars-afflicted aspects. Taylor's Mars forms a square to Burton's Mercury. This aspect causes disagreement, friction, and irritation. The female may be unconsciously identifying with her animus figure and as a result may attempt to overpower the intellect part of herself that she sees symbolized in the male. She may act and react instinctually, perceiving his thoughts as stimulants rather than ideas. As a result, the male experiences a lack of communication. In the Mars opposite Neptune aspect, Taylor again will confront identification with the male animus. This conflict becomes difficult to bring to the surface. The female sees images and dreams of herself in the male and tries to lead the relationship. At the same time, the male tries to escape from her dominance. Mars has a tendency to cause isolation while Neptune symbolizes energy that could blend into both identities. This aspect tends to cause some sexual conflict as well as a confusion of direction. The female might feel as if the rug were constantly being pulled out from under her, while her mate would feel that her desires are a constant interruption to his creative flow.

Burton's Mars forms a square to Taylor's Saturn. In this aspect, he seeks to formulate his individual identity, unconsciously struggling with memories of his father and the structured force of the superego that he feels he must overcome if he is to mean anything to himself. In the one aspect where Burton feels the strength of Mars, he must struggle with the oppressive force of her Saturn. He might feel like a little boy under the dominion of superiors whose expectations he could probably never meet. This does not allow a relationship to develop easily.

The final two aspects specifically show the struggle with fame. Burton's Jupiter forms an opposition to Taylor's Pluto. His sense of fame and honor would be in conflict with her appeal to mass consciousness. Her Jupiter squares his Saturn and shows the struggle between her fame and his ideas of tradition.

Karma

Was this relationship based on personal growth or was some specific karma involved? All partnerships afford an opportunity for growth. In the Burton-Taylor example we see how much each partner could evolve spiritually by overcoming obstacles, changing them into stepping stones that could be used to develop a deeper and a richer understanding of life. But the reasons for the relationship do not end here. With Taylor's Saturn in Aquarius forming a conjunction to Burton's South Node in Capricorn there are strong karmic implications. She comes out of his past to remind him of an obligation that had long since been forgotten. The South Node in the sixth house indicates obligations and with Saturn forming a conjunction to it, past life burdens must be shared in this relationship.

Both partners have their Nodes in opposite houses (the sixth and twelfth). Both partners have Saturn in the fourth house. Both have second house Moons. This tells us something. The sixth house represents the completion of the lower hemisphere of the chart. The twelfth house shows the fulfillment of the upper hemisphere. In a sense then, both horoscopes have south Nodes which represent areas of experience that should have been completed in a past life. If the karma was completed, each would begin a new karma through the North Node. Because they have opposite house Nodes, the North Node of each reflects a house experience similar to the South Node of the other. As a result, the relationship brings each partner back to consciously realize what was unfinished in the past.

Taylor's North Node (or highest area of expression in the current life) is in Pisces, whose ruler, Neptune, is the leading planet in Burton's chart. Her South Node is in Virgo; Burton has a Virgo Moon. This offers a clue to a karma having to do with Mother (Moon) and child (Mercury—ruler of Virgo). With both Saturns in the fourth house, there are current-life family responsibilities as well as burdens felt during childhood that serve to remind both individuals of the importance of the family structure. Here, too, we see a basic magnetism towards parental figures, home and family traditions. The fourth house rules *mother* but it also symbolizes the roots of the soul. Interestingly enough, it forms an opposition to the tenth house of career; a rather difficult placement for two individuals whose respective careers came to be so expansive and consuming. The fourth house emphasis would remind both partners of a karmic instance in their eternal past on some unconscious level.

Taylor's Saturn in Aquarius in her fourth house forms the conjunction to Burton's South Node. The karmic burden she brings him in this life is a family matter from another incarnation. Thus, the most difficult areas in their relationship would center around the establishing of a family. When the same conjunction is viewed through Richard Burton's chart, the sixth house of obligation, dharma, health and working conditions comes into the picture. Many of the strengths and weaknesses in this relationship are dependent upon their ability to balance the obligations of working conditions, health, and maintaining the structure of a family unit.

Interestingly enough, the powerful connections to the Nodes show that no matter who each partner is married to, the karmic relationship between them continues to be a source of inspiration and conflict to them both.

Conclusion

A person cannot see himself in a running stream; he can only reflect clearly in calm waters. For this reason we choose relationships so we can find a settling place in our journey through life. Passing emotions change too quickly for us so we look for the steadiness of an enduring relationship.

From moment to moment there are changes within a realm of no change. Slight ripples don't disturb the smooth surface of a lasting relationship. They provide the color and texture through which one grows.

All that we can learn spiritually has little effect on us until we are able to apply it to daily life. We cannot live on a mountain, isolate ourselves from the world and prove that our spiritual rules work. It is only through our day to day efforts to understand and love another that our spirituality surfaces.

We cannot all find personal or even impersonal greatness in the world. We can find *contentment* with our own personal greatness in the way that we relate to another.

To conquer or master ourselves is indeed an admirable life goal. To experience such mastery in the company of loving another is by far a better achievement. Spirit can take us high. Problems can bring us low. Neither the highest nor the lowest places afford the balanced stream of consciousness that is our true reflection. Our thoughts are never completely right, nor are they completely wrong. If we try to autonomously achieve spiritual greatness, we can never know the truth. We may see the words or ideas of the masters; we may even feel these words are true. We will never know for sure until we are able to reflect in the calm waters of a clear stream.

The essence of a relationship becomes the proof, the validation, and the confirmation of one's reality. If learning how to sincerely love another, regardless of the obstacles, is the greatest lesson in this Earth School, could we be here for a greater reason?